CHILD OF SORROW

To Dearest Helen

Love and Best Wishes

Patrick J Fahy

1 Nov 2009

by

PATRICK J. FAHY

authorHOUSE®

AuthorHouse™ UK Ltd.
500 Avebury Boulevard
Central Milton Keynes, MK9 2BE
www.authorhouse.co.uk
Phone: 08001974150

First published by AuthorHouse 9/28/2009

ISBN: 1-9781-4389-2122-8 (sc)
ISBN: 1-9781-4389-2128-0 (hc)

Printed in the United States of America
Bloomington, Indiana

This book is printed on acid-free paper.

INTRODUCTION

THIS BOOK IS DEDICATED TO MY LOVELY DAUGHTERS, who have always supported me one hundred percent, Eileen and Deirdre. To my lovely three granddaughters, Chloe, Shannon and Kyla. They give me the love and strength to get through the lonely and most vulnerable times in my every day life. I hope that by writing of my life experiences in the most human way possible, that people who make decisions on children's lives should also consider the whole life of the child and not something to hurry and get done with, as soon as possible.

The decision they make on behalf of the child if they get it wrong means years of mental torture and suffering for that child, of complete loneliness and isolation they have to endure every day they live. Every employment form you have to fill out through your life is a nightmare even if you join the Armed Forces. The filling in of Baptism forms, wedding marriage certificates, certificates of birth, give you such little hope of securing what you wish to achieve as your personal details are on display to everyone and judgement is often based on your personal details and not the person themselves.

As I signed the wedding register, with witnesses of people, I would not want to know of my personal circumstances, including my wife's sisters and husbands and my Best Man Peter Kelly and Mary his wife, all of whom I was too ashamed to tell my private life. All my private details were on display in the church and I was so humiliated. What I felt then I can't describe. I wanted it to be over as quickly as possible. Bernadette's sisters paid for all the food and drink of the day. I could not wait till we got back to our flat in Stamford Hill and be alone with her. The next day was Sunday. I went to Mass on my own. We did not have a honeymoon as I was on the lowest wages of that time. I had to pay for my wedding suit and shoes by weekly instalments. Peter Kelly was by Best Man, one of Bernadette's sisters was bridesmaid. I was back at work on the Monday morning and I worked long hours for £5 per day. I was never paid any extra for any extra hours I worked. My life at that time in 1971 was all work and nothing else seemed to matter. I did not know anything of women, of women's period time; I was totally ignorant of such things. When Bernadette told me she was pregnant one day after three months together I still did not understand what life was about.

John and Teresa, and Teresa's family were my true friends. John paid for all the travelling expenses. Put me up for several holidays, went searching for any family I might have had. As for Bernadette I am truly sorry I might and could have been better to her. I did not know any better way to behave as the system I went through, you were at the lowest form of education and ignorance and I certainly thank her for our two lovely girls and our three lovely granddaughters.

Patrick

THE FIRST EVER MEMORY IN MY LIFE WAS I WAS sitting in a house with a lady with a red coat. I had this memory several times of this lady and knew I was loved. The next ever present memory, the pony and trap had stopped. I could hear a lot of talking but obviously I had no idea what was happening. I was four and a half years old and had arrived at St Patrick's, Kells Road, Kilkenny. I remember that exact moment to this day. I was frozen with the cold and hungry, and knew something bad was to happen to me. Then I remembered my Holy Communion Day, seven years old, because I was wearing a medal with red silk. I did feel happy that day.

The memories of Kilkenny Orphanage are of hunger and cold. I knew every leaf and plant that grew and knew their tastes. I remember I was taken to the bathroom, half-naked but for a night shirt, one night to await a beating from the Reverend Mother Baptist because of something I had done. I still remember that beating (nine years old) to this day. I went to see the Reverend Mother on my departure with the 34th Battalion to the Congo in 1961. She was then working in a hospital in Dublin. I did not feel any hatred for her but wanted to see what she looked like. I think I felt both a mixture of pity and sorrow.

Anyway my stay in Kilkenny ended in September 1949 at nine and a half years of age. The first two years I had spent a lot of time in the hospital, St Luke's, Kilkenny City. I had learned from the nuns that my mother had died giving me birth so I was on my own. I remember a Brother Ryan coming to the bus station to pick me up and another boy called Roger Doyle. As we walked from Brians Cross, it was about two and a half miles of boreens to the school, St Patrick's, Upton, Co Cork, and it was raining. We passed the head teachers house, then past the Boys Graveyard, up a long avenue of high trees that seemed to go on forever. There was a sports field on the left and fields of crops on the right.

The fields of crops were to be my main nourishment for the next six and a half years, plus the cow shed. I used to steal mangles from the cows, such was the hunger we had to endure. St Patrick's, Upton was a hell from hell, is the only way I could describe it. It was run in a two-tier system, the boys from Dublin, Cork and Limerick were given the job of being Prefects in charge of us without mums and dads. Many a hiding I got for no reason other than I was an orphan. The Brothers never took any notice of any of this. The school was ruled without love of any kind being shown. It was a total fearful existence. Whenever I go to Lourdes, I go to the sheepfold at Bartrès and try somehow to share with Bernadette her time as a child and my own in Upton. We had to do all the farm work at Upton, 12 years of age, setting the potatoes, carrots, turnips, and in the autumn, picking the crops and pulling the flax.

At fourteen they put me into the shoemakers shop. I had to learn how to repair and make shoes. I hated the job and was no good whatsoever at it, but the choice was not mine. Bernie Kirwan, RIP, was a very fair man, always treated me well, as he did all the other boys.

We had two Brothers in charge of us, Brother Johnston and Brother O'Brian. To be as fair as I can I don't think they had any proper training for the job they had taken on. They ruled the school with so much fear and often at times children went missing from their trades, sometimes for hours on end, and they would come back black and blue from beatings they had received. Every time they were returned you were in great fear that it might be your turn next. We never had any warm clothes, no underwear whatsoever. We were constantly starving. I used to duck out of the playground and steal the vegetables, eat the dirt off with my teeth and eat the wild crab apples. From my time at Kilkenny I knew every leaf and the trees with the best leaves, and how they all tasted differently.

During my time in Upton one of the Prefects, who were looking after us, I was about 13 years old at the time and was very ill with flu and the Brothers and all the children had gone to Mass. The Prefect was from Dublin and he tried to put his excitment in my bum. Even though he hit me several times I would not let him do it. I could not report him as he said he would give me a real hiding and I was afraid to tell the Brothers in case they might beat me.

During our time in Upton the boys, who were sent from Dublin, Cork and Limerick, would go back to their parents for four weeks holiday. About half of the school was left and would go to summer camp. The Brothers attitude during these holidays would be very friendly, and even some glimpses of love emerged.

I stayed at Castle Freke near Rosscarbery, Clonakilty in 1950. I was taken very seriously ill and do not expect to make it. There was a priest, Father Fennell, who looked after me, fed me, washed me and made my bed. Whenever I awoke he was sitting on a chair beside my bed reading his prayer book, always putting cold towels on my forehead. I think it was about ten days before I finally recovered and I still remember that time. I can't see his face but know he kept me alive and saved my life

Then in 1954 we were at another holiday camp in Garrettstown, not far from Clonakilty. The Brothers took about 20 children swimming but had not checked the dangerous tides. We were not long swimming in the sea when a great swell of water came upon us. Where it was about a foot deep, it was suddenly six feet deep. There was a boy not far from me, Hugh

O'Brien. He was shouting for help. I went over to him, offered him my hand and stayed with him for a few minutes. He was panic stricken and was lashing out with his hands. Then he was gone. I struggled back to safety and when I reached shore I found out the Brothers had saved about ten children. Hugh thankfully was washed ashore and lived but one of the boys did drown. I don't know if my actions on that day were right or wrong. We never had any swimming lessons. Maybe if we had I might have helped Hugh better. I would have to admit even now I would do the same under the same circumstances. I would again respond no differently. I have often thought of that day, sometimes of guilt, and sometimes the fact that I did go over to him to offer my help but could not deal with the situation better.

I will always remember Upton as a hell on earth. I have visited it twice since leaving in 1956, in 1991 and 2006 with Marie, mother's sister's daughter and her three beautiful daughters. In February 1956 a farmer from Milltown, Near Killorglin, Co Kerry arrived at Upton who was sent to pick me up. He had a cattle lorry full of cattle. It was snowing heavily that night. Mr O'Shea was his name.

We arrived at Mr McGough's Public House in Milltown about one o'clock in the morning. Mrs McGough made me Galtee cheese sandwiches. They had three children, Terence, Mary and Bartholomew, the new baby. Mr McGough was a kind man but the very first day he put me to work. He had a pub, pigs and cattle and tried to be a shoe repairer. I was useless to him so he decided he would return me to Upton. I did plead with him not to send me back; I would do anything. At 6am I fed the pigs, carried the turf, about a quarter of a mile away, chopped the kindling and did whatever they wished. They gave me great food. I received a shilling on the first Sunday of every month.

I was a babysitter to Bartholomew and brought him everywhere with me. I used to walk the pram every morning to Maggie Murphy for the milk and the same again in the evening. She used to live with her nephew and had one cow. Maggie was so good to me. She would give me big slices of her homemade bread, full of butter on the top. Her favourite song was the 'Rose of Mooncoin' and she taught me all the words. She was the first person after leaving Upton that gave me love. I went up one night for the milk and Maggie had done a homemade loaf for Mrs McGough. It was still on the fire baking. Maggie was sitting in her favourite chair. I said 'Maggie', but she was already dead. I was frightened.

I remember Maggie's funeral the next day, all the village had drawn their curtains as the four black horses pulled the hearse. I still remember her loving kindness to me. Maggie was about 84 then, used to walk to the village most days, and back, about two and a half miles each way.

I got so much love from Bartholomew. He was like a brother to me. Mrs McGough could not understand me, or I her. One of my most embarrassing times was I used to share the same bed with Terence. She would come into the bedroom every night to tuck Terence in. I did not get any underwear at Upton so you can imagine my humiliation night after night I had to endure with lots of reference, 'We don't know who he is, or where he's from'. I did not know at this time of any family connections. Her children were very kind to me but I can understand Mrs McGough's concern for her children.

Then in September 1956 I was carrying bags of turf from the shed. They would get a full lorry delivered. I was on about the third bag to the house when I fell on the cobblestones, which were filled with pigs waste, and broke my left leg. The pain was excruciating. I would stay awake all night crying. No notice was taken of me by either Mr or Mrs McGough. I was limping but I carried on with my work as best as I could. Some of the children used to come up behind me, while I was pushing Bartholomew, and give me a kicking up the bum. I had to accept it all in humiliation. They would laugh as they ran away, 'Look at the boy from the Home'.

At Christmas 1956 Mr McGough at last believed that something was wrong with me. Dr Sheehan was the doctor in Milltown and I went to see him. He sent me to County Hospital in Tralee. The doctor in Tralee asked me what happened, and when I told him it happened in September and that I continued working he said, 'I don't know if we can save the leg. You should have come to us at the time it happened. You have to go to St Finbarr's in Cork City. There's a Doctor O'Connell there who might be able to help you'. Mr & Mrs McGough showered me with kindness then. Mr McGough's brother John, who used to work at Fords in Luton, was over for the Christmas and drove me back to Upton. I was in severe pain and crying most of the time. One of the Brothers, Brother Keenan, took me to St Finbarr's where I met Dr O'Connell. He did suggest amputation at one point, which I did not know what it meant, and agreed. I went back to Upton at 17 years of age. I was a problem for them. A broken leg, no home, no job. At the hospital they put my leg in irons from my thigh to my heel and issued me with crutches.

I stayed in Upton for ten more weeks and then Brother Keenan said I have found you a job in Cork City, in the Grand Parade. You will be staying with Mrs Ryan and her son Frank in 12 Cook Street, Cork. They have a shoe repair shop in the Grand Parade but you have to give up the crutches or you won't get the job and be near the hospital. I felt so humiliated, walking and limping, around the Grand Parade carrying shoes, being a messenger boy as well as all the other duties.

Mrs Ryan was very good to me, like a mother, but I had to convince Frank, her son, I was worth giving a chance to. I did my best to please him, which was not easy. He did become great friends with me but it took a lot of time. I was on my feet from eight o'clock in the morning till 9pm most nights. The leg was not as painful as it was so I took the irons off, and bit by bit, I managed without the crutches or irons. I knew then I had conquered one affliction. I was going to join the army at 18 years of age. It was in my heart and soul.

Teresa Coleman worked in Ryan's with me, my best friend at that time. She was so beautiful I was in awe. Teresa brought me to her home. Her sisters Noreen, Patricia, Maureen, and her brother Finnbarr were to be my family for eight years. Her dad, John, and her mum, Hannah, were mum and dad to me at 41 Connolly Road, Ballyphehane. I used to go there every Sunday for dinner, play King of Spades and 45. John O'Connor was going out with Teresa and they now have five beautiful children. Gus Harrington, Cork All Ireland Player, Manager of St Finbarr's Football Club, used to go out with Pat. The happiness this family gave to me cannot be measured. John O'Connor was later to play a very important part in my life. I have had holidays in Crosshaven, with John and Teresa, in Myrtleville in the last few years. We often talk of those times.

I stayed at Ryan's shoe shop until I was 18, and although she begged me to stay she said if the army don't take you, which I doubt very much, I will keep the job and your room for you for a month.

I JOINED THE IRISH ARMY ON MY 18TH BIRTHDAY, 8th day of March 1958 after leaving Ryan's shoe factory the day before. I limped up to the Collins Barracks, with great doubt, whether I would be accepted or not. I was let into the Barracks and granted a medical to see if I was fit or not and to fill in all necessary documentation. At that time the army were in full recruitment and means of joining up were not of the strictest code that they could have, and would have been, at other times. I had to strip naked, and after a thorough examination and x-rays etc, the medical officer asked me why I was limping. I told him I was playing hurling and got injured. He was a keen GAA man and sent me to the Commanding Officer, 4th Southern Battalion, Cork to say had passed my medical A1. I was then sent to the Quartermaster stores to receive my uniform boots, rifle and fatigues.

I was then taken to one of the billets for new recruits. We were to undertake six months of square bashing parade after parade. We had to endure trips to the rifle ranges at Kilworth and Youghal, also grenade throwing, but always with an officer present, a few times to see mortar shells exploding. During this time the men in this platoon were good to me, knew I had no family, and if found out with a broken leg, I would be instantly dismissed and have no job or place to go to.

Mrs Ryan, 12 Cook Street, Cork City let me stay in the small room at the top of the house, 6x3, with a skylight. The bed just about fitted in there. She let me have breakfast, dinner etc and in return I would bring her a bottle of Sandeman Port, polish the sitting room lino every Friday night and Saturday wash the kitchen, toilet, stairs and hallway. She was very good to me, as was Frank Ryan, her remaining son.

She had a daughter Mary who was married to a policeman in Scotland Yard. They had a daughter, Patricia Stanbridge. I used to love them coming to Cook Street on holidays. Patricia was beautiful, the first girl my heart went out to. She had a special friend, Mary Lou Harding. I was living at that time with two beautiful girls. Patricia went on and married later to an English Ambassador. I did meet up with them a few months later and was to keep acquainted with them for some years on.

As like all army personnel the first six months is the hardest of all. Most of the lads I joined up with were from Co Cork or Munster Province. There was a Corporal Higgins and Sergeant Bruno Walsh from a little island a few miles from Cork City. Sergeant Walsh and I hit it off right from the start. He taught me how to shoot, and I was quite good by the time he was finished with me.

I passed out my recruitment in September 1958. After special leave, I was back in Collins Barracks again by October 1958. We were training to go to the interment camp in the Curragh of Kildare where all the IRA prisoners were held. I was posted there with most of the lads I had done my training with. As it was winter it was freezing. We had to go up on raised platforms with sentry boxes on each corner, and in the middle section watch these men continuously walk one-way system below us. As I had learned all my years in school all the brave deeds of the IRA, I could not understand why we were keeping them prisoners. I had taken the ultimate oath for Ireland so I would honour that commitment whatever but I had my doubts.

There was a mass breakout attempt later, before the Christmas 1958, and I was in the search party looking for the internees. We saw a group of men running through the Curragh fields. One of the lads shouted to the NCO Sergeant what he saw. The sergeant led us in the opposite direction. Right or wrong I was so relieved as I don't think I could have fired on them if ordered to, after all they were Irishmen as well, and the IRA were my heroes.

We returned to Cork before Christmas after six weeks at the Curragh. It was lovely to be back in Cork. I stayed in Mrs Ryan's house that Christmas and I also had a very strong friendship with the girl at the counter at Ryan's shoe factory in the Grand Parade, Teresa Coleman. Her family were to be a big part of my life forever from 1957 to 1964. I spent most of my weekends with the family. Teresa, Noreen, Patricia Finnbarr and the baby Maureen. Their parents, John and Hannah, were so good to me, as if I was one of them. The pub trips and the card games we used to enjoy are still a wonderful memory for me. I still correspond with them even now in 2008 and have had several holidays in Myrtleville near Crosshaven, Co Cork where they still live.

After Christmas I was assigned to the shoe repair shop in the barracks with Jim Browne, Paddy Gorman, Joe Wright and Corporal Bill Dunne, the barrack's tailor. I was to stay in the shop as it kept me off guard duty for two and a half years. Then in 1960 I would have finished my first three years in the army. I wanted to go back to civilian life but at that time, December 1960, we had heard of the life in the Congo, the chance of making and saving a lot of money. I was always so poor and broke most of the time. We used to get three pound, two shillings and a penny per week. I think at that time my pay would have been about £7 a week (1961).

I signed up again and rejoined the army. We had to go on serious training for the hope of being selected for the Congo. My leg was still not a hundred percent healed but it was getting better with all the route marches and heavy training, including all night route marches. The 32nd Battalion and the 33rd Battalion were nearing the end of their term of duty in the Congo (1960) and the army asked for more volunteers for the Congo. I volunteered and had all the major injections, malaria and all others that went into getting ready. The names of the new B Company for the 34th went up in the canteen just outside the adjutant's office. A Captain Fitzgibbon was adjutant then; he was from Youghal. He certainly did not like me. He had a son named Peter who was to be my Parish Priest some years later in Abbey Wood and was to baptise one of my daughters. He was a very shrewd man and sensed, and knew, I had a problem with my left leg. I knew at that moment he was the person who chose the men to go to the Congo. After all the training and receiving the injections etc I was not to be selected. I cried my eyes out as I watched the jubilation of the men selected. I was going to leave the army March 1961 as I felt I would never get a chance of going there while Captain Fitzgibbon was adjutant.

We had Christmas 1960, the last annual leave before the 34th Battalion left for the Congo. The lads were all excited to be going to Dublin ready to fly out to the Congo. I was not even on the reserves list. They were to leave on the Monday for Dublin. Then the barrack Quartermaster called me on Friday evening. I always got on really well with him. With men in the 32nd Battalion and 33rd Battalion and now the 34th Battalion leaving I felt really down. There was hardly anyone left in the barracks when the married men went home at 4.30. Then the barrack Quartermaster said to me, 'Private Fahy, would you like to go to the Congo? You have had all the training and you will be going as the boot repairer with B Coy attached to the HQ Company, 34th Irish Battalion'. I felt on top of the world that moment but kept a very low profile because with all the parades etc Cork, Curragh, Dublin and all the top army and civilians of Ireland watching including the

Taoiseach, Sean Lemass. There I thought I still may be found out and would not be allowed to go.

When I finally got on the Globe Master, the crew were all American. They loved the Irish and we felt so easy and happy in their company. There was all strap seating and an upstairs deck as well if you wanted to sleep. Not very comfortable but I had my dream trip to the Congo come true and nothing else mattered. We knew about ten words of Swahili learnt, and we arrived in the Congo in bulls wool uniforms, leather leggins, green web pouches for ammo. Point 303 rifles ammunition, later Gustav, was only issued on guard duty and patrol duty. We were to be stationed at Kamina air base.

Our first stop from Ireland was via Sabena to Brussels, then onto Kano in Nigeria. It was the very first time, not one of us had seen a black person before in our lives. When the waiters came over to serve us dinner we could not stop looking at them. From Kano we went onto Wheelus American Air Base in Tripoli, then onto Léopoldville and then to Kamina.

Some, or most, of our duties in the 34th were at Camp Ruwi, Kamina Air Base, Elizabethville Airport, and we had to stay about six weeks in Luena. We lived at a train station in Luena, stayed and lived on the train for nearly six weeks. We met several English and Belgian mercenaries. A few surrendered themselves to us so they would get free passage back to their original country. There was a big leper camp in that area, which was out of bounds to us. The Swedish troops used to guard this camp and had great big Alsatian dogs; they were quite vicious. They did not like the Congoleese and I don't think they had much time for us either.

During our days in the 34th we had only the old British Ferret armoured car. Later with the Swedish troops, somehow we began to get most of their armoured cars, which were much bigger and safer, and with much superior firepower. During the final six weeks of the 34th Battalion we were stationed at Elizabethville Airport. The discipline was so severe. If on guard duty at the airport we looked anywhere but in front of us we were put on a charge. Our clothes had to be pressed and boots polished – as all the brass parts of our equipment had to be shining. If any officer or other important civilian person passed by and you failed to present arms you were also put on a charge. It was so stressful that I was glad when the tour ended.

During my time with the 34th I met and made two great friends, one was John Drake. John was very bad with the reading and writing. As I got very few letters myself from Ireland, only from John Coleman, Teresa's dad, I did all the reading and writing for John. He had nine in his family, two girls and seven boys. They still live at Sarsfield Terrace, Youghal. John invited me back to stay with him in Youghal. I became great friends with Helen his sister but could not bring myself to tell her or her family that I had not a family of my own, that my mother had died giving me birth. I loved Helen. I would have married her but with the terrible reminder I had spent six and a half years in Upton, I fled the scene. I still kept in touch throughout my life.

The other was a little Congoleese boy called Antonius. Like most of the Irish lads we all had a favourite child who would wash and press our uniforms, do all the chores and get coal for the iron as we had no electricity. He always had two great bubbles under his nose and only a short pair of trousers he wore as his clothing. Antonius had learning from the Missionary Priests. As I knew all the Latin Mass by heart and as I was in the choir in Upton so Antonius knew it as well. We would sing all the Latin Mass together. It brought a special bond between us. I used to give him half of my dinner every day and sometimes I would bring him 7Up from the canteen. I used to go over to his commune and play football with the children. I always trusted and loved him as if he were part of me. When we went into the last few days of my tour I stole blankets etc for him and his family, gave them what clothes and Congoleese money I had left. I hugged and kissed him, but I was glad to be going back to Ireland.

I saw Antonius in tears on the runway as we took off for Ireland not knowing, or thinking, I would never see him again. There was also a Congoleese girl of 13 that lived in the same commune Josephine. She also was a great friend. Even though we could not understand the language we used to have great laughs. Antonius used to live on the commune nearest Elizabethville Airport. I have often thought of him during the years after I finished with the 34th. It was a great learning for us, as part of us growing up. I still remember the Congoleese girl of about 12 or so taking her own baby from herself. The very next day she was in the field digging for food. The Congoleese were a lovely people and had a great sense of humour. Whenever I was in their company I never feared for my safety or felt threatened by them, even when I was unarmed and in their company on my own.

I was told of what happened at Niemba because we went there one Sunday with the 4th Battalion Pipe Band from Cork, most of whom I knew personally. We brought presents from the Red Cross and other charities. We played for hours all the Irish songs for the Baluba tribesmen, played football, chatted and made friends with the children. I got the impression from them that they were genuine in their sorrow for what happened at Niemba, but that most of the Irish were wearing the same clothes as the former Belgian Army wore, and they did not know the difference, as they were all white. Lots of the stories I had heard from other Congoleese men convinced me they were speaking the truth as when I arrived first in the Congo we also had problems with our uniforms. Like all of us in the Irish Army at that time we were shocked to learn, and to feel the same sorrow as members of their families did. We all mourned to see the river crossing where it all happened. I could imagine me being in the same patrol; may they all rest in peace.

We arrived back in Collins Barracks sometime in June 1961. All the parents of the men B Company were at the Barracks to greet their sons. Most of the men's mums and dads, brothers and sisters, sweethearts were there to greet us like heroes. Then I felt alone after all the euphoria. Mr Coleman was the only one who welcomed me. John Drake's dad and mum, Anita and Helen, sisters, were there for John. John said to his mum could Paddy come back with us home. They knew of me through all the letters I had written for John. I stayed with them through the first two weeks of leave.

We got a month off, 42 American dollars and £10 in Irish money. I never had so much money in my life, and what with six months back pay, I felt like a millionaire. During our time in the Congo we got paid in Congoleese francs so all our money back home was put in the bank for us for our return. John's dad, James, and mum, Kitty, were like mum and dad to me. They did all my laundry. We used to go to the Clock Tower in Youghal and Kathy Barry's Chubby Checker was in full swing, and then I had the bonus of Helen. She was a lovely person and one, if not the biggest, regrets of my life. I had not the courage or direction to hang in there. I had tasted family life as never before and had the company of a lovely girl. There was no an ounce of sense in my head, I lost it all.

I went back to Mrs Ryan at 12 Cook Street, Cork. I felt so lonely after that holiday with John's family. Mrs Ryan and Frank her son welcomed me. I used to meet some of the lads who were in the Congo and lived in Cork. We would go for a drink sometimes.

Then the leave period was over and we went back to the Barracks.

I was then sent to Spike Island, one officer with a few men to be a temporary boot repairer. After two weeks I was then sent to the Irish Navy for two months to help another boot repairer at the naval base at Haulbowline. Hitler Healy was the name of the man. I got on really well with him even though I was a useless repairer. He would ask me to do other work and polish the boots; a very nice person.

Then in October 1961 the Irish Army were looking for volunteers to go out to the Congo, especially anyone who had been out there previously. I volunteered and left Haulbowline, launch to Cobh, then by train to Glanmire Station, and walked up the hill three miles to Collins Barracks. Because of the late date, October '61, the Cork Battalion was already full so they sent me to Sarsfield Barracks in Limerick. I was to be part of No 5 Platoon B Company 36th Irish Battalion. I knew only three of these men. One was Corporal Harney PA MP, another was Dennis Murphy from Cork City, and the other was Corporal Brennan, a signals man from Limerick. I was to be carrying spare ammunition for Private Nick McQuaid who was the section Bren gunner. Most of this platoon were from Limerick and Tipperary. Lieutenant Larry Kiely was boss, Sergeant Jerry Short was Co-Sergeant. We had Corporal Harvey, Corporal Cyril Sweeny and Corporal John Geogheagan.

During November and December we were training at the Blackwater River, Fermoy and Kilworth, we had to cross a river with heavy pack and rifle, climb onto a rope and cross the river. I made three attempts, after a quarter way across I fell in each time. We had army divers to rescue us so I was rescued three times. Some of the lads made it across. They gave me a pass certificate because I had at least made the effort. In December we then set out for the Congo our plane broke down in Tripoli. The American Air force gave us

VIP treatment. They allowed us into their PX and clubs on the base. First time I experienced hot water of the Mediterranean. We had no knowledge of the situation in the Congo, but we were shocked as we were landing in Elizabethville. About 5.30pm in the evening there were flashes of thunder and lightening, heavy machine gun fire, mortars etc. The Globemasters never turned their engines off. We arrived at Elizabethville and the fear of God was on me. If it was possible there and then I would have gone back to Ireland. What was to follow was a nightmare. We were never informed of anything, the only thing we were to know was to follow the last order given. To think that the man who was at war with us was the very same man I was bodyguard for on a UN ANC patrol a few months earlier.

When I had seen President Tshombe in person for the very first time he wore a suit of shimmering gold. There was so much gold on his person. His plane refuelled at Elizabethville as he had to go somewhere. As I was on guard duty that day they had to quickly form a UN patrol with a large UN flag on the jeep to accompany him to his destination. So he had his own troops plus four UN soldiers so he could get there are quickly and safely as possible. About five hours later we arrived back at the airport. Heavy boxes were also loaded on. He shook hands with the officer that was on duty, waved at us and thanked us. I was never to see him again in the 36th Battalion.

That night we went outside a remote area of Elizabethville, Rousseau Farm, where we met lots of the 35th Irish Battalion. Many of whom were at the siege of Jadotville. I was talking to some of these men when a barrage of mortar bombs etc descended on us. One minute its daylight in the Congo, next second its pitch dark. Everyone took cover. The 35th Battalion had dug massive trenches all around the farm. The exchange of shells and machine guns continued all night. I was never so glad to see the morning, but also sad to see the 35th go off in trucks to go home. I wished I was one of them. I went into a trench with Corporal Brennan and Dennis Murphy. We were on the corner trench that was to be our home for the next twenty-three days. There were the armoured squadron right behind us. I think we were as much afraid of getting hit by them as the mercenary army. They would let go with bursts firing over our heads every few minutes. Then a return fire from the mercenaries. I prayed every minute to God during these weeks. It was a constant headache to be in fear of dying at any second. Trees were falling everywhere around us and our greatest fear of all was to see hundreds of rounds of red tracer bullets coming at you. I don't know how many times I changed my trousers but I did every time I got the chance.

The food each day was a small tin of Argentine bully beef, four Jacobs's biscuits and a bottle of soda water. No water at all was available. The soda water was used for your teeth, shaving and washing your face. Usually they would be a lull in the shooting by both sides from about 8am to 3pm in the afternoon and you could go to the toilet etc. The armoured cars used to bring the food to each trench. Just as you would be inclined to relax a sniper would start shooting at us and we would have to go back to our trenches again. Every minute you expected to be attacked as they were an all or nothing fighting men. They were fighting for a life that was very rich. Most had been born in the Congo so to them they were fighting for their country. We had no political motive to be there. Whatever our reasons for joining the army we did not know who our enemy was. One day we would share the airport guard with them or Camp Ruwi or Kolwezi or wherever we were told to go. I could not make head or tail of anything. The man on sentry duty with me today would be firing at me tomorrow and I would return fire.

Then one evening the army Chaplain and Commandant Callaghan OC B Company said tonight we are marching and we are going to take the tunnel at Elizabethville, and then to take Elizabethville if possible. The Chaplain said I will give you all general absolution. We said some prayers and then Commandant Callaghan spoke to each platoon officers and NCOs. They told us there may not be many survivors and if anyone was to let down the company they could go back, guard the Rousseau Farm, and they would have done the company proud. Anyone that was to do the march had the strictest instructions not to open fire at any time under any circumstances. If the person in front was hit you just carried on walking, not looking left or right. There were Swedish armoured cars a mile behind us covering our backs which depended on us getting to a certain position at the right time the head UN Military Commander had planned. Anyone of the UN personnel that came under fire had to deal with the problem themselves. The success of the operation depended on each company officer.

I was with Lieutenant Kiely 5 Platoon officer and one sergeant (Jerry Short) who was always singing Helen Shapiro's song 'Walking Back to Happiness', three NCOs and 18 men. I followed Private Bill Nooman. He was in his thirties and a lovely person who guided and looked after me during this terrible time. 'Paddy' he said to me, 'keep looking at the back of my head. Remember they have to hit me first before they hit you'. A very brave man. I wet myself several times during the march to Elizabethville; the mortars and the sight of red tracer coming at you. I was very religious at that time and I thought I would be meeting God that very night. I prayed when it came to die I would not let the platoon down. Lieutenant Kiely was very brave as if he was on a route march in Ireland.

As he said by the left quick march no one word was spoken by anyone as we went closer and closer to Elizabethville.

The shooting and noise of machine gun fire grew louder and louder each second. Then we reached the crossroads and a parade of shops which was our destination, ready for the big drive the next morning. At dawn the next day the fighter planes gave a pounding on Elizabethville and the tunnel area. By 11 o'clock we had orders to dig in, which meant digging trenches all around the crossroads, with orders no-one comes through. We had to protect that crossroads as it was the last route through to the tunnel leading through to Elizabethville. We had no food at all that day, or water. Then some Swedish snipers came towards us. At one time we thought they were mercenaries and were ready to shoot them, then we recognised the UN badges. They told us the tunnel was secure and the Irish Battalion had done its work very well, and that they thought that the white mercenary soldiers had surrendered and there was talk of peace within the next few days.

Bill Noonan and myself shared every guard duty. He kept me in one piece, always giving me advice. I hope if I ever meet Bill again I will say a big thank you to him. At our crossroads there were thousands of bags of white flour that previous troops used as sandbags or other to protect themselves. They were stacked high so you could stand up behind them and shoot. We could see the local native commune from our position. These innocent people had suffered the same bombardment as we had. They had not get any food or water for several weeks. I was on guard behind the bags, and I think it was Christmas Eve or Christmas Day 1961, with one section of S Platoon. I was then in charge of the Bren gun and I kept it well oiled, and I always looked after it because one day it might save my life. All of a sudden there was a charge of Congoleese men, women and children running in panic towards us. I was waiting for the order to fire. There were several shots. Corporal Geogheagan said lads move out, let them have the flour. He had deliberately walked in front of us to stop us from shooting. It was sheer panic as at that moment we thought we were being attacked but all the people wanted was the flour. The bravery of this action by the Corporal saved all our lives. Imagine if he had told us to fire, we would all have been killed. So many natives and then no ammo left, they would have torn us to pieces. Corporal Geogheagan was killed in friendly fire. He was a shrewd solider and he put his life at risk at that time to save his section. He died in hospital a few days later.

Within ten minutes or so all the flour bags were gone. The Congoleese people ate from the bags on the ground with their bare hands. They were not in the least concerned about us or the guns but of sheer starvation. They had to have food. I did think this was to be my last day. One of the many heroic deeds I witnessed from my fellow soldiers. I thank God, as I was ready loaded with the Bren gun, safety catch off. I was so scared but held my fire. If Corporal Geogheagan had not ran in front of us I would have fired and it would have been a massacre of innocent people. When we moved away from the parade of shops, two of the lads carried the Corporal. He was bleeding in the stomach. Then lots of UN soldiers came on the scene. We were so lucky to leave that situation alive. I went back to the villa we had taken over, looked at the Corporal's bed knowing he was seriously wounded, could die. I had only known him about six weeks in all. He died giving his life so other raw soldiers could live. I think of him all through my life. If I only had a part of his courage, RIP.

The situation in the Congo became peaceful again after the Elizabethville and tunnel onslaught. The City of Elizabethville was like a scene from the Omega Man, all the houses, shops and factories were deserted. No 5 Platoon had four or five roads, all with beautiful villas to search, as had all the other platoons and company's their own areas to clear. We were under great stress at this time as the Belgian mercenaries would kill us if given the chance so we did a house by house search, bayonet on the tip of the FN. It was such a big area to clear and so often or not we would be on our own. We had instructions to shoot if doubtful. I was about an hour into the house search, my FN rifle already loaded, primed to shoot. I burst in the door, shouted 'Anybody in here?' Then I heard crying from one of the bedrooms. I froze, ready to shoot. Then I saw a young girl who was lying under one of the beds shivering and afraid. She must have thought I was going to shoot her. I told her I was from the UN and I would take her to my officer. I felt so sorry for her. She had stayed under the bed for nearly a week. Her parents owned a photographic shop in Elizabethville and they had gone without her as they did not know where she was. She could only speak French and I could only speak English so I had to escort her back to my officer with her hands over her head, and I holding a loaded FN behind her. Not much bravery there, but we had the strictest instructions not to trust any of the white population. I got her back to the UN officer and interpreter. The poor girl had not eaten in days. They fed her, and as I turned to go back to continue searching the houses and villas she ran up to me. She was so beautiful. She kissed me full on the lips. The interpreter said, 'She says thank you for saving her life. She was afraid she would be raped and killed by the ANC'. She was crying with relief that she was safe and to see her family again. I think she would have been about 19 years old. I returned to duty to continue clearing the villas, some of which had been looted, everything gone. We took over the best villas and slept on the floors, sometimes with six mattresses in the one room.

Most of the days after we cleared the houses. They were rich in food supply so we carried all the food we could to the villa we were in. The shops and warehouses were full to the brim, VAT 69, every drink imaginable was there packed to the ceilings. The clothing warehouses were fully stocked. One day alone I changed my shirt eight times. I used to give anything I did not want to the Congoleese people in the commune. We were great friends. Then one morning, I had come off guard duty, the worst time of a soldier's life as you are so tired and just want to go to bed. This little boy came running towards me, 'Paddy, Paddy'. The bubbles were still under his nose, he was crying his heart out. I hugged him and kissed him. It was Antonius I knew from the 34th Battalion. I never thought I would ever see him again. Antonius was to do all my washing and share my dinner every day. He was my best ever friend in my life and for the last four months of my duty with the 36th my saviour.

Most of the Irish lads had their favourites. I think I got the true friendship of a human being. I know if it ever came to caring for Africa or its people it was Antonius I would see every time. So loyal, brave and his lovely smile I will always remember. He treated and respected me as no other person had done and I think would have done anything for me. I did the same for him and his family as I had done in the 34th, nicked blankets, whatever I could for him. Then it was goodbye for ever. I think of Antonius all my life, of the wars he has had to live through, all his every day turmoil, and that of his family. In some ways I could have been born of his family. I would not mind at all and would have been proud to be part of that family.

Most of our duty in the 36th was at the crossroads into Elizabethville. The swimming pool every Sunday was a luxury. Each week we all would get our day. The lovely girl I found in the villa came back to see me several times. I met her parents. She always gave me cartons of 200 cigarettes. She used to even come to our villa. We would get special leave for about four hours and pick me up to go to her shop in Elizabethville and we would have dinner at her parent's house. She took my photograph and sent it to the Belgian interpreter Mr Roger's at the crossroads. It is a reminder of those days. Like the Congoleese people, there was genuine white people who cared for the Congoleese and had only their goodwill in their hearts. They suffered the horror of war, the loss of loved ones, their homes, and their country as many had been born in the Congo, and had had to go and live in exile forever.

If anyone has any knowledge of Africa, it is the most beautiful of all countries in the World, with its natural beauty. As I walked around Elizabethville I saw for the very first time banana trees and mango trees. It was so breathtaking, like I was in another world. There were tree after tree of bananas. How could the people have no food? There was food here in surplus. During the last few months of my 36th Battalion tour I met lads from Cork, Tipperary and Limerick. We did not know one another before the tour. I saw every day heroism from these men. I was on my second tour, some had just left school. They were the true soul of Ireland and through them I survived.

We went on patrol to areas where no white persons had ever been, to people who had never seen white people before, or the ones they saw were not in friendship, white mercenaries, that they showed so much fear and hatred of them.

Lieutenant Kiely, such a brave officer on the march to Elizabethville, such coolness and bravery in front of a platoon of men, hastily gathered together at the very last moment, to Sergeant Gerry Shortt, ever a fan of Helen Shapiro, taking everything in his stride.

To Corporal Geogheagan, his bravery and example in front of thousands of refugees out of control. To Lieutenant Tommy Dunne of Limerick. If Lieutenant Dunne had not been present at this particular incident friendly fire would have trebled the losses we had at Niemba. I don't think any army tribute to him was awarded. I was there that day ready to open fire. He stood up with everybody shooting at one another, calmed the situation down and no-one was hurt. I had cocked my Bren gun and would have started shooting but for Lieutenant Dunne. I would not have had the courage to do what he did that day. We were in an abandoned ANC Barracks. We were all in different areas. Someone opened fire, not knowing there was another Irish patrol nearby. It would have been a tragedy for us all if anyone had died like this. Lieutenant Dunne prevented one of the most patented tragedies of all time by his coolness and bravery. I had only briefly met him before this time and rarely saw him again. I only write and know he could easily have died with lots of live ammunition flying around. He stood up amid all the shooting, shouting 'stop firing at one another'. He rescued us all that day. Lots of soldiers have died in friendly fire. Lieutenant Tommy Dunne prevented us doing the same to one another.

The 36th Battalion No 5 Platoon from the first minute of landing. Some or most had not been to the Congo before. I had been with the 34th so had more experience than some of these men; to have to spend night after night in trenches on their arrival in the Congo. All the 36th Irish Battalion took part in the fight for the tunnel and Elizabethville, as did the Indians, Pakistanis, Tunisians, Moroccans, Malayans, Danish, Swedish and Ethiopians. All of these UN forces laid their lives down. We all had to depend on one another to be at a certain position at a certain time. Every nation that took part were all heroes as one could not have survived without the commitment of the other.

The Moroccans were my favourite people. I often would meet with their men and share our country and their country's views. We were all young men and shared much of the same ideals. I was very lucky to have been left a wealth of memories of such men. I was and am so proud of our A Company in the way they fought for the tunnel. We were there supporting them. They were the heroes that night. Some on that night had given the ultimate and died in the service of their beloved UN and country. I think their effort that night, as all the UN troops who took part at the tunnel and Elizabethville. We got rid of the mercenary soldiers from the Congo forever. The UN should always be proud of that battle – all strangers fighting for the cause of Freedom of Africa, and free its people of years of poverty and slavery. I do hope the UN remains with the vocations it had in 1961. So many countries youngest men coming together to fight for peace and to put their lives on the line in the sincerest service of all.

I returned to Ireland around June 1961. As most of the lads were from Limerick and Tipperary. I was stationed in Cork. I never met any of them ever again. I was going out with Kathleen Galvin. Kathleen was from Lotabeg Mayfield. Her dad, Davey, used to work at Ryan's shoe factory. Her brother Mick was a great person; loved the Guinness. I have had many a great night at the Liberty Pub with most of her family. Kathleen and I went out together for nearly two years. She was the most trustworthy girl a young man could find. I told her all of my history, of everything I was. She was not bothered by any of it. All her family accepted me. I used to go out with her sisters and their boyfriends, attended a few weddings, but I could not forget my own problems and I thought and knew Kathleen deserved a better person. It was something I could not get out of my mind, it was blocking my happiness, and her happiness, and I knew that it would be wrong to ask her to marry me. Her sisters and brother all married, I did not think myself worthy of Kathleen as I thought of Helen before her.

I told Kathleen of my decision and fell into despair. I went down to Mrs Ryan, ever a friend, to listen to me on breaking up with Kathleen. Mrs Ryan and Frank, the shoe factory, was in debt. I gave Frank my Congo money to get him out of trouble and because of what his mum had done for me. This was one of the darkest years of my life. I gave up my Kathleen. I last heard from her in 2003 in Ontario, Canada. She has four young men. I am so happy for her.

Anyway I returned to Collins Barracks, Cork, July 1962. I had about £100 left in the bank. I thought and hoped I would get another tour in the Congo. Then one of the most important people came into my life. It was Captain Eamonn Young. The Captain was a famous football All Ireland Player for Cork. I knew his brother, Doctor Jim Young, himself a Cork hurler and won a Cork All Ireland Place. I used to fill in for Eamonn when he had a session of squash booked with his brother at Collins Barracks and could not make it. Once I cut Jim's forehead with a whack from my squash racket. I used to treat him, Eamonn, as a hero and gazed at him in awe. One day he said to me, 'Fahy, you were in the Congo a few times tell me about it. I am going out as the Commander of B Company, 39th Battalion. Lieutenant W Edgar is one of my platoon commanders you will be with him'. I told him of the times I was so afraid. I was completely honest with him in everything, of being not belonging to any family and my time spent in Upton, and that maybe I might let him down if there was any fighting. 'Fahy, report to Lieutenant Edgar Monday morning, you will be part of the 39th Battalion and part of my company, B Company. I will talk to you again in the Congo'. He was good to his word. Many times he would come to me during our tour with the 39th, always gave me praise I did not deserve.

The gap between officer and private was so huge, the level of difference in that year was so awesome, you only got to talk to an officer if you were on charge or were saluting after being paid, and asking for a weekend pass. Commandant Eamonn Young broke all those barriers down. He was the most human being I had met in my life. He was a hero footballer and a senior officer in the army. He used to ask me to play squash with him and his brother Jim. I was the lowest private in the army, a nobody with no family, no money. 'Now Fahy, I have not come to the squash court for nothing, I want you to try your best to beat me. You are younger than me'. I never beat him or Jim as hard as I tried. We often showered together and afterwards he would say to me, 'You are getting better but try to be more aggressive'.

I won the Cork Squash Novice Championship that year. As I was joyfully presented with the trophy he never said a word but smiled at me. I knew what it meant. During my 39th Battalion Tour of Duty with Lieutenant W Edgar's Platoon he wanted us to be free and express ourselves as often as possible.

We were on patrol to show local villages of our presence in that particular area and at about 11 o'clock we reached a river. It was a very humid day. Without any warning he took off all his clothes and ran into the river. Everyone wanted to swim and we all just followed him into the river. After about ten minutes in the water, 'Crocodiles' somebody shouted. I never saw so many white bums running from the water. Commandant Young and Lieutenant W Edgar, as officers, the gap between men, would could die on the same patrol, had narrowed so dramatically. The respect for each other was mutual, Commandant Young for me during patrols of which I was a part. His versions to the Congoleese people of the 'Scottish soldier', 'jug of punch', and Brennan on the Moor always remain with me. I still hear his voice, a true son of Dunmanway and Cork, and Ireland.

During that tour Corporal W Graham, our Section Corporal, was sent up to a remote former Belgian golf course along with Private Tony Aldrid, Mickey Quirke, Tony Cassidy, Tony Moone and I. The nearest civilisation was about 60 miles away. We were dropped in by helicopter. After a couple of weeks there Corporal Graham said we only had tins of beef and Jacobs biscuits. There were two UN officers coming in by helicopter that Sunday. We drew lots to see who would go into the nearest village to buy chicken or hens or goat, or whatever, so we would have a good meal for the officers. I won the prize of going to the village. I told Corporal Graham I would not take any weapons as the Congoleese might have concerns and not trust me. The village was about three miles away. I only had shorts on and snake boots, and 100 francs for whatever I could get. I followed the dirt track and met lots of women on the way, Jambo, Balli Gani and other Swahili greetings. I finally arrived in a village. The Chief, and the people could not have been friendlier or nicer to me. They brought out the local brews, Simba Lion and Tempo Elephant were the two local brews, of Belgian brews, about one and a half pint bottles. I told them I wanted to buy meat food as we had not eaten any fresh for months. I gave them 100 francs and they tied up a goat for me. 'But first have a drink and a meal with us'. They used to say a European could only drink two bottles. After five bottles of Simba and Tempo, the village people laughed at me as I got drunker. But they came back with me to our camp with the goat pucking at the back of my legs. They thought it was so funny. They could have at any time taken my life. I had no gun, no money, nothing, but they fed me, gave me all the Simba and Tempo I wanted and looked after me. I sang the 'Banks of My Own Lovely Lee', probably never heard of again in that area. They were lovely people. To a white person, who came in peace and friendship, they gave their all. The beautiful girls danced for me, the children sat on my lap, the men came and clasped my hand. I could have lived with them forever.

Corporal Graham did the necessary and we had the goat meal with the officers that Sunday. When Corporal Graham told them I had gone to the village unarmed and alone and that the village people had cared and all the hospitality they had shown me, they told us the Belgian troops used to go there at night and open fire. If they hit somebody that was bad luck. That was one of the ways they subdued the villages of the Congo. Those people that carried out such evil deeds on such innocent people have to one day face God, need I say more.

I have travelled thousands of miles on patrol throughout the Congo. Its people are from Heaven, like Antonius, Josephine, like the village people who did not know me or where I came from, trusted me with their children. We could not understand each others language but we knew we were friends. I was part of their life for three Tours or more but I know I am part of it forever. Some of the elder's might still remember me. The 39th Battalion was my last Congo trip. Commandant Young, Lieutenant W Edgar we were on patrol. We hope we gave to the Congo that not all white people are bad.

I have many memories of the Congo, its people and the many personal encounters I have had with this people. My own men in the 34th, 36th and 39th Battalions, of the training before each trip, the training at the Blackwater, Kilworth Fermoy and the Curragh Training Camp, and in Dublin. Whatever my life was worth, the men I lived and worked within the army, especially in my Congo years, I feel so proud that I served with and lived with them during those years.

Of the many friends I met of the UN, of the Congoleese people I met, especially Antonius, President Tshombe, who I met briefly, of the lovely French girl I rescued from the villa, of some ANC people I had to return fire on. To heroes, like those of A Company 36th Battalion, of all Geogheagan's S Platoon, of many of these Battalions where no-one saw their brave deeds. This is one of the heartaches a soldier has to live with. Captain McAllister when one of the sentries opened fire while he was checking his own troops. Corporal Geoghegan was looking out for his men. So many heroic deeds I saw and witnessed from Irishmen in the Congo. Some had never fired a rifle only on a shooting range in Fermoy, Youghal or Kilworth. Their targets in a few weeks would be a mercenary army who hated a UN Peace Keeping Force. I try to imagine their side of the conflict. I slept in their villas, swam in their swimming pools, drank in their clubs and bars, but at the end of the day it's the Congoleese people's land, not theirs, like Ireland. We had oppression from England. I am with the Congoleese people's side. No country should rule over what's not theirs.

During my six years in the army, as most young men, we had differences of opinion and sometimes it needed sorting. Sometimes we would fight with fists but once we did it was forgotten about and we would be friends again. One particular problem I had was with a man from Cork City. He was Munster Boxing Champion as well as being All Army Champion. He was always trying to ridicule me in front of the other platoon men. Like when we were leaving Dublin for the Congo. When saying goodbye to family and friends, everyone was crying. He said 'Fahy, what are you crying for, you have no-one to cry for?' Some of the men would laugh at his remarks. He was a nasty piece of work. One afternoon we had just had a medical, we had a medical inspection every week by the medical officer. We had to stand to attention by our beds naked. He would then look at our penis to see if we had caught any disease from the local native girls. If we had an problems we would have to report to the medical orderly on a daily basis. We were cleaning our rifles and equipment, ready to go out on a several day patrol. He started his remarks to me again. The whole platoon was there including two of the NCOs. I took him by the collar of his shirt, asked him to come outside and fight me man to man. I told him I would keep hitting him until he begged for mercy. He would not accept the offer to fight. I told him if he ever put those remarks in my direction again. The billet was in total silence as I told him I would put a round in my FN rifle and blow his head off. He suddenly went pale and collapsed on the bed. He never again spoke to me, would nod his head to me, and I would do the same in his direction. He treated everyone with total respect for the remainder of the tour. Would I have carried out my threat? Yes, without hesitation. I had nearly three months of taunts from that man. No-one ever talked or spoke of that incident. Even the NCOs respected me more from that day. They knew he had crossed the line, gave me the benefit of doubt, and did not report it on file. I got a total apology from the man himself which I accepted. God must have looked after me and prevented me from a deed so evil I don't know what direction my life would have gone. I would have let my men down and, of course, Lieutenant Bill Edgar and most of all my commanding officer who had do so much for me, Commandant Eamonn Young.

We went out on patrol for nearly ten days, all was forgotten. We had happy days at Kalwezi. I used to run the Pitch & Putt Club. We had to put 50 francs in the pot, winner took all. It was a great success. Then we had poker tournaments. We did our own concerts, a little bit like Dad's Army. You always got characters in the army. I had one argument with one of the Congoleese men. He was a bit flash. He came around to the camp, selling what he had claimed were uncut diamonds. They could be used in a jeweller shop in Ireland and would fetch a good price. He had done this to several of the lads. I said nothing to anyone and put a full magazine in my FN. I went down to the village on my own. I had given him 1,000 francs for a few pieces of worthless glass, as had the other lads. I found him at last. I cocked my rifle and asked him for the money he took from me and the lads that day. At first he started to say it was not him but I recognised him and told him he had a minute of his life left. He handed over all the money. If you show up at our camp again I will remember you. You are not welcome and stay away. None of the Congoleese moved. They knew what he had done and they respected me. I was very lucky that the man did not come back to the camp and complain. I would have been sent back in disgrace to Ireland. Most of the village knew of my time with Antonius and that I fed their children whenever possible. Whatever happened after I left the village I don't know. I never saw this man again.

I returned to camp, did not say a word to anybody of what I had done or where I had been. I had gone back for my 1,000 francs, a month's money in the Congo, right or wrong, from a cheating person. I often met the people from the village after that incident. They were their usual friendly selves and I think they even respected me all the more. I did not feel proud of what had happened but sometimes in your life you do something you are ashamed of. This is one of those things I should have let go. I did not and it could have been nasty, all for a very small sum of money. I have regretted it since.

After the 39th Battalion I could have gone on. I had been picked for Nicosia in Cyprus. I felt it time to go, see the world.

EXTRA SPECIAL TRIBUTE TO ARMOUR SQUADRON 36TH BATTALION

A SPECIAL TRIBUTE SHOULD GO TO THE MEN of the X British armour car who saved my life at Rousseau Farm. Sergeant John Cooke was in that squadron. I have talked to him of it but he does identify hearing of it. He says not his crew.

I had left my trench to go to the canteen. I'd taken a chance as I had no cigarettes or drink. I did not take my rifle with me as I thought it would only take me a few minutes up and down. I had bought two tins, 50 sweet Afton, one tin of 50 Gold Flake and as much 7UP as I could carry. I only had shorts on and black boots. I was almost back to my trench when a shot rang out. I could feel it go by my head. In the Congo there are dykes on both sides of the road, especially on a farming estate. I jumped into the nearest dyke; it was full of stagnant repulsive water. I threw up several times as well as filling my shorts. I began to move along the dyke towards camp. After about 100 yards I looked out to see what was going on. Another shot rang out. I was in a sniper's sight. I threw all my cigs etc away. The smell was so bad. I kept on discharging at both ends. I could not even return fire. I kept thinking of God, please help me. It was the longest half an hour I had ever spent in my life. I knew if I put my head up again I would be dead. Then an Irish armoured car came along. One of the men was on the turret with a twin Vickers machine gun.

He spotted me, stopped the armour car, opened the back door of the car and let go with several bursts of fire towards where the direction I though the sniper was. They brought me back to camp. I could not wait to get out of my clothes. I know the crew of that car saved my life that day. To them it was an every day patrol. As they said 'Routine patrol'. I was grateful to that routine patrol.

I go to UN weekends in Tipperary some years and I meet children of some who died at Niemba. I go with Irish UN and ONET veterans. When we say our prayers for other soldiers at the Cenotaph on Remembrance Sunday I still think of that crew of the Irish 36th. But for them I would not be at any Remembrance Parade. God be with them.

LAST YEAR IN CORK

I LEFT THE ARMY IN 1964 AFTER TURNING down the offer of a trip to Nicosia in Cyprus. As I had lived all my life up to then in institutions I wanted to try out something different. I had about £350 in the bank then and decided I would try to open a business myself. I looked around Cork and nearby villages. I decided I would open a shoe shop as that was the only trade I knew something of. I rented a shop in Blarney Village and stayed with Mrs Looney from Monday to Friday. She had three boys, Tom, Aiden and Ray, and a daughter, Catherine. Ray used to help me in the shop and take me fishing to the woods in Blarney. I bought a finishing machine and all the tools I needed. Mrs Looney's husband had died on a cycle tour of Ireland, a well-known cyclist in the 1950's. Even though she was wheelchair bound she treated me like one of her own children. Sometimes we never get to repay a person in our life that has been so kind to us. Mrs Looney and Ray were exactly that to me. Ray was a young looking Elvis Presley. Anything I asked of him he would do. Sadly after I had gone to England a few months Ray had passed away without me ever knowing. I have gone back there recently and met Mrs Looney and Catherine, as well as meeting Aidan, who has a bicycle shop in the North Main Street Bridge.

Mr Batty O'Leary, who I rented the shop from in Blarney, was a very fair man and after six months in Blarney the business was going nowhere and when Teresa and John came out to see how I was doing, along with Sheila and Barry Ahern. Barry used to play in the Dukes show band, a great friend in those days, as was Sheila and all her family. I had spent nearly £200 to keep me going and I decided to quit and try something else. I went to see Batty O'Leary that Monday. He helped me to get a buyer for the stuff in the shop and charged me no rent while it remained there. I said goodbye to Blarney and I got a job the following Monday with Tedcastle McCormicks. I used to go to a pub in the South Main Street, the Liberty Bar, so I knew the three Harris brothers over the years. I would work mostly in the boat holds filling the skips with coal. If you did not go to the pub after work you would not get a shift the next day as you got paid daily. This is what I did until Christmas 1964. I had great fun with the lads who worked on the coal, but working all day, and then drinking until 9pm every night I decided that Christmas I would try my luck in England. I told Mrs Ryan of my intentions. She was so disappointed I was going but knew I would not change my mind. I said goodbye to her February 1965.

I went to the National Provincial Bank in Patrick Street and left £10 in the account in case I would need it in Cork again. Little did I know I would not see Cork again until 1991. Cork City will always be special to me. If I was born the best person in the world I would also like to have been born in Cork. I have many good memories of Cork people, like the Coleman family from Ballyphehane, the Galvin family from Mayfield, the Drake family from Youghal, the Linnane family from the Old Youghal Road, and of course, Mrs Martha Ryan that took me from Upton with a broken leg and was my adopted mother. Whenever I had no money in my years in the army she would always lend me, and if meeting on a date with Kathleen would say, 'How much do you need?' Always was strict with me as regards to money. She knew I had no sense whatsoever. My army days in Collins Barracks and, of course, my Congo days I might have never had if I did not meet her. I promised I would go to her grave.

She died in Guys Hospital a short time after I came to London. I have not gone back as yet. Please God in the next few weeks.

I went back to see if my account in the bank was still alive but nothing was found.

I SAILED FROM CORK CITY 1965 AFTER EXPERIENCING great frustration and not knowing any direction in which to go on with life. I said goodbye to Mrs Ryan at 12 Cook Street. I don't think she or anybody else in Cork at that time could care less. I met a Mr Brown on the boat Innisfallen. I was at the time so naïve and I trusted him completely and agreed to go with him to Finsbury Park where he said we could easily get a flat. On arriving at Paddington Station we, or I, paid for a room at Sussex Gardens, Paddington.

After a lovely breakfast, I used to smoke then, and after buying cigarettes for Mr Brown and I, we got the tube to Finsbury Park. I had never seen so many people on one train. The girl opposite me was very beautiful and such as was my thinking; I'd hoped I might see her again and ask her out. I did not at that time think there were hundreds of those trains every hour passing through to so many main stations. I never cast eyes on that lovely girl again.

We arrived at Finsbury Park Station. There was a house owned by the Catholic Church at Stroud Green Road. We stayed the Saturday, Sunday and Monday nights. We had Mass and Rosary before we went to bed. On Tuesday we set out looking for a flat of our own. Mr Brown found one in Adolphus Road, Finsbury Park. I paid the £15 rent for two weeks. The rest of the week I paid for the food, kettle, saucepans, Delphi knives and forks and all the food. Mr Brown said there would be no problem getting a job. I signed on at the Labour Exchange, Medina Road.

I had the experience of working in the shoe factory so I set out for work. I walked from Finsbury Park to Tottenham Court Road to a shoe factory called Harts, opposite University College Hospital. They told me I could start the following Monday. I got back to the flat that Friday night and paid for cigarettes and for Mr Brown's girlfriend, including cinema, Saturday, Sunday, plus all the food for that weekend.

It was a very severe winter that time. The fare from Finsbury Park to Tottenham Court Road was 10d. The snow was so heavy that parts of London were 2ft, and higher. I went to work that Monday morning at Harts shoe factory. By 11 o'clock the manager told me I was of no use to him, or the factory. I broke down in tears. He felt so sorry for me that he put me on inking, that's when you put brown ink on the brown shoes, and black ink on the black one's, then you have to polish them on a finishing machine. The better shine on the shoes, the better the customer was satisfied. After a very difficult day, and nearly losing my job on the very first day, I set back home to Finsbury Park expecting Mr Brown to have some food cooked. It was absolutely freezing and snowing very heavily. I arrived back at the flat and the door was wide open. I pressed the light switch but no light came on. It was only then I noticed the meters for gas and electric were both broken into. They were both sixpenny meters. I had a box of Swan matches and lit one so I could see. Then I noticed my suitcases, all my clothes, shoes, polish, my toothbrush, and even my comb, were gone. Even my pyjamas were gone. I had suits from the Congo and even my Congo medals. My UN beret and badge were gone. All the spare money that was to keep us till we got work was gone.

I shivered with the cold as the flat had no central heating. I cried and cried. I did not know what to do or how to deal with this situation. I was starving, freezing and in a country I did not know anyone. I did not have a penny. I went upstairs as there were two Nigerian students living there. They could not help me but allowed me to ring my landlord and let him know what had happened. Mr Davies, a Welshman, arrived and I got all his verbals. He threatened to call the police. I promised him, with eyes full of tears, I would pay him back every penny that was taken from the meters. He said as the weather was so severe he would let me stay until Friday but if I did not pay another week's rent in advance, plus the money from the meters, I was out on the street. On that Friday I received £8.17 shillings and he took from me £8.10 shillings. I still owed him £2.18 shillings which he said he would expect the next Thursday. I bought two large loaves of bread and a packet of cigarettes, milk and that was to be the last food for another week.

On Saturday morning I set off by foot to go to Arlington Road Catholic Church, near Camden Town as one friendly Irishman told me to go while the priest was willing to hear my confession. He told me if he was to give £5 to everyone who came over from Ireland he would be sacked by his bishop. I left Arlington Road that Saturday and passed Irish pubs and betting shops. I was too proud and stupid. I would not ask for help. I arrived back to the flat Saturday night and threw all the blankets from Mr Brown's bed, and my own on top of me. It was so cold, so much snow outside, you did not need lights on in the flat. I threw all the bedclothes over me with all my clothes and shoes on and fell asleep.

I got up Sunday morning, no wash or shave, or clean clothes. I went to St Gabriel's at Tollington Park; I never miss Mass. As the collection man came up he whispered in my ear, 'Mate, you stink. Could you please go to the back of the church?' I did as requested then he said, 'And please don't go to Holy Communion or the people will leave the church'. I did as the man asked. As I was going down the steps from the church, I only had my working clothes, no overcoat, and starving, and so cold, the snow was beginning to fall again. I had asked Jesus, if possible, please help me, at Mass that morning. I felt I must be the lowest person in the world. Then as I went to go back to my flat a voice called out. 'Here mate, can I have a word with you? How did you get into such a state?' I looked around, it was the collection man from the church. I told him what had happened, the meeting of Mr Brown on the boat and what happened, and that Mr Brown had taken everything belonging to me. He told me, 'Be down at my house, 34 Osborne Road, Finsbury Park by two o'clock. I will have a bit of dinner for you'.

As I walked the streets of Finsbury Park the snow was now heavier than at eleven o'clock. I was so cold and numb, I was going to pass on the dinner. However, I did go to 34 Osborne but I had so much snow on my hair you could not see how dirty or unshaven I was. I rang the doorbell and a lovely girl came to the door. 'What do you want? I have no money'. I said the man from the church told me to call for some dinner. 'You wait there, he has not told me'. I went to walk away from the gate of the house, to go back to the flat and the man ran after me. 'Marie did not mean what she said. We have a month old son, David, so we have to be very careful who we bring in our house. Please come in and have dinner with us'. I was so grateful for that dinner. Tom McCrory, a British Rail Inspector, gave me his clothes, underwear and socks. After a bath, I had then been ten days without washing, I felt so vibrant, so wonderful. It was nearly five o'clock and Marie made me some sandwiches for that evening. She told me her brother served in the Congo the same time as I had served. It broke down all the barriers. I now had friends. Marie said come back to our house tomorrow night and we will have a room ready for you for £2.10 shillings a week. I paid Mr Davies what I owed and then stayed with Tom and Marie and David, done babysitting for them, for about 18 months. The lesson from Tom I got was if a person goes to Mass, whatever he looks like or smells like can't be a bad person. Tom that morning he met me looked on me with compassion. I hope people I meet, or have to meet, I look on them with the same compassion. God is in us all if we want him to be. In the greatest hours of despair he always seems to thread a path to me.

Tom was from Co Tyrone and Marie from Drogheda, Co Louth. I hope David has had a good life if he ever reads this. Tom probably saved my life and my heart belongs to him and Marie. I stayed with Tom and Marie for 18 months. Then I was working on the new Victoria Line. I moved from Finsbury Park to Tottenham High Road and became great friends with Peter Kelly. He was sharing a house with his girlfriend and two girls from Ireland. At his invitation I moved in as well. I met Mrs Abraham, a Polish refugee. She was very good to us so I had company for the first time since I left Ireland. For about £3 a week she did all the bed linen, shirts and underwear, socks etc. I was very happy that year and went everywhere with Peter and Mary. Peter and Mary decided to get married and I was Peter's Best Man. Then I met Peter's sister, Kathy, who was married to Joe, so I was building a genuine circle of friends from Peter's family. Then Peter said he was moving out of Mrs Abrahams, Ruskin Road, and would I get a place with them. I got a single room in the same house. Peter and Mary had the flat in the same house so Mary used to cook my dinners.

A few months went by and little Gerald was born to them, followed by Caroline a year later. We were almost one family. I would look after the children when they wanted a night out. Sometimes Kathy would come down, or we would all go out together. I was foreman on a building site for a firm called Ready Placed Concrete. I had a disagreement with one of the lads on the site. He had two brothers and one Sunday after Mass, while I was waiting for Mary to call me to dinner, the two brothers, big men, who had come originally from Dublin, knocked on my room door. 'You had a problem with our brother'. With that they laid into me for sometime and smashed my record player, the only valuable I had. 'Any more problems with you at work we will be back again'. When Peter called me later I told him what had happened. He said there was a gang of them of about eight, all from Dublin, and some of them carried knives as they knew Peter was my best friend. I told Mary because of the children it would be better if I left and got another place to live. I went up to the Prince of Wales Hospital. They had broken my nose, knocked a few teeth out and hit me on the back of the head with such force it broke the only chair in the room. With blood all over my head and face, my suit and shirt, I waited for treatment at the hospital. An Irish girl cleaned me up, I was in shock. That night I stayed in my boss's yard in a store shed. I never met Peter or Mary for years later.

The next morning my boss arrived at the yard and when he saw the state of me he said you can't go to work in that state and you can't stay here in the yard either. The man who I had the disagreement with arrived a few minutes later and he sacked him on the spot. He came over to me to tell me how sorry it happened and could I get his job back for him. I asked my boss, an Englishman, John Bastin who used to live in Harlow New Town. He said 'Paddy, have you looked in a mirror this morning? I will never employ that man or any of his brothers who did this to you'. I felt sorry for Martin as he had a young wife and needed that job badly. I told him what the boss said and that I did ask for his job back. I never saw him again in my life.

At that time I used to go to Arsenal one Saturday and then the next Saturday I would go to Tottenham Hotspur, White Hart Lane, followed by a few beers in a pub called the Corner Pin. I knew Dave MacKay, John Robertson, Alan Gilzean and the great Jimmy Greaves almost on a personal acquaintance. I also worked at Bobby Moore's house.

At the earliest chance I set about looking for another place to live. There was a George Molloy who was a carpenter for Mr Bastin my boss. His wife's name was Francis and they let me stay with them for a while until I got a place. She had a sister called Bernadette, who was later to become my wife. Francis and Bernadette's dad were going back to Kilkee that week and he wanted £100 for the lease of his flat and all the furniture etc. I borrowed the money from my boss. The flat was great. It had five bedrooms but I had to give a room to Kevin, his son, who had a girlfriend called Anita from Kilrush, Kilkee. I don't know why but Kevin never took his Wellingtons off while in bed with Anita. They never seemed to be out of bed at all. If you ever went into their bedroom Kevin's Wellies would always be sticking out at the bottom of the bed. I think Anita liked him wearing them. That flat was in Colsterworth Road, off Tottenham High Road.

I recovered from the beating and then I got Kevin a job with Mr Bastin. A great worker and friend, always a great laugh, and we bonded really well. 'Pat', he said to me one day, I was 26 years old then, 'why don't you get a girlfriend for yourself and get married? You don't want to be on your own all your life. I have two twin sisters, Martha and Bernadette. They are staying with Francis at Station Road. Why don't you come with me to the Loyola Hall Sunday night and meet them and my mother?' I went with Kevin that Sunday night. The girls were very beautiful and I instantly fell for Martha. She told me to get lost as I fell very short of her expectations.

As I used to go to bed alone I could hear Kevin and Anita screaming with joy. I think they used to overdo it just to get me going. I would think of Martha. It was the first time in my life I began wanting a girl with all my heart, it's the truth. Martha would hardly look at me but she came to the Royal at Tottenham, an English Dance Hall. Frank and Nancy Sinatra had a song out then called 'Something Stupid'. As I danced with Martha during that number I never felt so awkward. I thought the pressure would undo all my buttons in my trousers. Martha must have realised it as well. 'I think you need to go to the toilet'. I took her home that night. I don't think she had any idea how much I fancied her and wanted to be with her. I think I was in love, real love for the first time in my life.

Martha returned to her nursing studies in Dublin and she said she would be staying there for two or three years. I did not see her again until her wedding day a few years later on when she married Brian, an Englishman. In the meantime I saw more of Bernadette, who had an on/off relationship with a lad called Jamie. Bernadette said to me, 'I will give Jamie up and marry you'. I replied back to her, 'You don't know anything about me. Maybe if you did you would have second thoughts'. Bernadette in her own way was very charming and I thought to myself what Kevin had said to me. 'You would have a wife and home to go to Pat, and maybe have a few children'. I thought about this for quite some time and agreed with Bernadette a day to marry. I told her of what had happened to me in Ireland, all the truth of everything. We would marry because it would be of advantage to her, and to me. We set the date. Bernadette at that time was living with another of her sisters, Doris, who had a partner called Bob, with two boys, James and Roger, and a two year old girl called Ellen. They were to be the most loving family to me. Bob was a lovely man from Michelstown in Cork. Doris was so good to me. I blended into her family and used to take the children to the park and build houses with them. That was a very happy life for me.

Bernadette and I married in April 1971. We lived in a Jewish flat in Dunsmure Road, Stamford Hill. The flat was haunted with a presence of a middle aged lady. As it was a furnished flat, and as I was making love to Bernadette, I looked above the bed. There was a photo, and my hair stood up on my head and a cold shiver went down my spine. I swear I saw the lady's eyes move. The next morning I told Bernadette and we took the picture down from the wall and put it down in the basement. The next night we heard a great crash from the basement. When I got there I never felt so frightened. The picture lay on the ground with all the glass lying scattered around the floor. I ran from there as fast as I could back to the bedroom with my heart pounding. I told Bernadette about the picture and all the glass on the floor. 'Pat, I have only a few weeks more until the baby is due, I want out of here'.

At that time I was working for Mr Stevens from Dagenham, a friend of Mr Bastin, my former boss. He just started a firm called Albills Concrete. They used to specialise in concrete pumping. Mr Stevens had seven sons. They used to live at Dagenham, and a boy from next door called Mr Flynn. Peter was a lovely man. Anyway Bill Stevens, he had a partner called Bill Jury, hence Albills, who was from New Zealand. When I joined them they said if I worked hard they would look after me. I worked some days 6am in the morning and was still working at 9pm as we had to rig pump pipes to the scaffolding, and after the pour, all the piles would have to be taken down, washed and put on the lorry ready for the next day. I worked all over the UK and while the company expanded and was making an absolute fortune my wages remained the same, £27.50p per week. I worked Saturdays and Sundays for free during the first two years; then the Thames Barrier Contract came up, 24 hours work a day, seven days a week. I decided that was enough for me.

I left Albills and found a firm called Brunells Constructions. There were three brothers from Bristol but originally from Cork. Paddy was a real card, then there was Michael and Don. My wages went up from £27.50 to £100 per week. That was for six days work. We built three blocks of flats off the 'Belvedere Hotel' near Belvedere Station. I was therefore 18 months. By that time I had also worked at Costains in Hailey Road, Belvedere. Most of the workmen came from Sheerness. They were nearly all Englishmen, a great bunch of men. I was very happy at that work during this time.

Bernadette had our second child who we called Deirdre. She was born 1974 in St Nicks Hospital, Plumstead High Street. I went up to the hospital in my Wellies and old clothes as I only got an hour off. They used to keep the mothers in the hospital for ten days until they fully recovered. Deirdre was so beautiful, 'A Little Angel'. During her childhood she was my rock. It did not matter what I said, or done, she always stood up for me and take my side if there was any arguments with Bernadette. Eileen was two years older. I had to beat her in every football match and even if I gave her a start of 9-0 I always beat her 10-9. Such was my skill. I took the girls everywhere with me. For the very first time in my life I had a family of my own.

Bernadette was very fiery and I used to travel all over the country with Albills, as I rejoined them again. Lots of times I would leave Monday morning and not be back again until Friday night or Saturday afternoon. She never told me she was unhappy with me or the job. I went on one job for Albills to Bridgwater, Somerset for three months. I had no full licence but often I would take the firm's lorry to Weston-Super-Mare and spend the time there as we used to start work 5am and finish at eleven o'clock. On one occasion I was driving back to the camp site and it was very dark. I did not know the area. I went up Clare Street, a one way street the wrong way, with lots of cars headlights trying to warn me. As I got to the car park I could hear police sirens everywhere. I got on top of the lorry, the police had three cars on the three entrances and I decided I would try to get back to camp via the one way street the opposite way. I left my lights off, free wheeled down the hill and made it back to the campsite and went straight into my caravan to await the sound of police sirens. They never came that night. I wonder how long they stayed at the entrances that night? The next morning I went to work as usual. Albills rang me from Belvedere about twelve o'clock to ask me what I had been up to the night before, that every police car in Bridgwater was out looking for their lorry. As I was the only person from their firm working in that area it must be me. I had to go down to the police station and tell them I had taken the lorry out without their permission. They threw the book at me and I received a criminal record for stealing the lorry. Even though I drove the lorry for several months prior to that day at that particular time the IRA were bombing the UK. While I did not approve of any of such deeds the police were very anti-Irish at that time so, rightly or wrongly, it had given me great satisfaction that I had got away that night. The court gave me a heavy fine and banned me for six months from driving any vehicle. I made my mind up then that I would either give up the drinking or driving altogether. I gave up the driving as I could easily have killed or injured an innocent person. I have only driven a bike since.

I left Albills for good then and I got a job with Costains on the Thames Barrier. I stayed there for 12 months. The work was so boring. We had to do three different shifts each week 7-3pm, 8pm till 11pm and then the third week 11pm until 7am the next morning.

There was a strike almost every week. Sometimes we would spend the whole shift playing cards in the canteen. I left them and decided I would try to set up on my own.

I met an Englishman, Alan Stiles, who I used to have a drink with in the Abbeymead Club. We bought a van and started looking for work. I was fairly good at the brickwork and I got a job with an Indian man I met while working for Brunells at Belvedere. I had to build him a laundry extension. I carried all the dig from the manhole 6ft 6" deep in his back garden through his house and filled three skips on the road outside his house. Then I had to carry all the bricks, cement and ballast up the six steps, through the house and into the back of the house. I had to do all the mixes myself, cut out a channel on the 10" pipe, and then build the manhole with steps. It took 1,400 bricks to get to the surface. Then I had to dig a trench from the house to the new manhole. I did all the labour work myself. Sometimes I would work until 11pm at night. Mohan always gave me dinner and whisky, and bring me home when the work was finished. I thought it very good work and I was proud. I asked him for £700 for the work and he said he would give me a cheque on the Monday. As Mohan and his family used to pray everyday, I used to see them on their knees almost every day, I trusted him, and also because I used to work with him. I called back four or five times the next two weeks and then I knew he had no intention of ever paying me. Bernadette gave me a hard time. I could not blame her as I had worked three weeks for nothing. I never saw Mohan after that, but I was on a train from Abbey Wood to London when one of his daughters got on the train bedside me. She did not recognise me, or maybe did not want to. I said to her, 'How could a family that prayed so much not pay me for the work?' I asked her if she would mention this to her father. I know it had nothing to do with her personally and told her so. That was the last time I saw any of Mohan's family.

Me and Alan picked up some work. We had to work very cheap as there was now a heavy recession in London. Then we got a job in Boxgrove Road, Abbey Wood, a complete new garden wall with a new slab floor. It did not turn out anything like it appeared in my head. As we put the floor slabs out the lady asked if we could put red cement in the joints. I got two packets of red dye from the builders yard. We had 45 gallon barrel and filled three-quarters with water. Alan went off to do another job and said he would be back to pick me up at 5pm that evening. I had no experience of dyes or anything so I opened the first pack of dye (red). I did not think it strong enough so I put the second packet into the water and after that I still did not think it red enough. I decided to go to the builders yard for some more dye. So I set off for the builders in Plumstead High Street.

It began to rain very heavily so I went into the Plume of Feathers. After two pints the rain stopped and I got the bus back to Boxgrove. The barrel of water had overflowed over the top with all the road full of red dye and quickly I ran upstairs to turn on the water hose. I began to wash down the road but all I was doing was spreading the dye even further. By this time the whole road, some 100 yards, all the pavements and the lady's front garden was a sea of red. The lady's beautiful Collie from Scotland, all his white coat was now red. The lady came out crying, 'Please go and turn off the water. You are only making things worse'. I ran upstairs and left a trail of red footprints all over her hallway and stairs. When I went to turn the hose pipe off there were two big red footprints on her daughters pillow so I turned it over. Then after turning the tap off I had left two more footprints on the other side of the pillow. I ran downstairs and by this time it was nearly 12 o'clock.

I had done no work. The lady was on the phone to her husband begging him to come home as she had a disaster on her hands. It began to rain again and the Collie was rolling all over the road and running into the sitting room of the house, jumping on the settee. The settee and carpets in the sitting room were now red as well, as well as the bedrooms quilts. By now Ron her husband, a fiery Scotsman had arrived home. 'What the F has happened?' I told him it was not anybody's fault as we did not think it was going to rain and they gave us the wrong dye. Later on in the afternoon, about four o'clock, Alan came back. I had no food or anything to drink. He took one look at the road and drove on. I was still trying to wash the road and pavements at 9pm. By that time the traffic had spread the dye right down Boxgrove Road. The traffic going the other way took it down Eynsham Drive, both ways. There was red everywhere. At 9.30 I told the family I would be back next morning to finish washing down. I went home to Bernadette. She said, 'Why are you red?' I had red hair, every part of my body and clothes washed. She told me to take off all my clothes and shoes as I had brought the red into our flat as well. She went berserk and threw my dinner in the bin. 'Did you get any money for me today?' Then I told her what had happened, and the dog, and about the road. 'You big F-ing idiot'. The next thing there was a knock on the door. It was Mrs Norris the lady, with her daughter. I kept saying sorry, it was an accident. Then the daughter said I saw the red boot marks on my pillow and when I turned it over there was more on the other side. Bernadette told me to clear off and leave the flat.

I went downstairs, we used to live at 8 Byland Close then, and saw Bert in the Pegasus Pub who subbed me a few pints and cigarettes. Then Alan came into the pub, laughing his head off. I said to him why did you not stop and help me. It was the joke of the pub and club for weeks after. I came back into the flat after 11.30 that night. Bernadette and the children had gone to bed. I ran the bath, then got into bed, I never wear clothes in bed, and Bernadette started asking me what was going to happen about the mess, then I fell asleep. The next morning I went back to the house with Alan. I told the people I would do the walls etc for free because of what had happened and we would get cleaning fluid to clean the road and pavements. The road and pavements were red for months after giving me a constant reminder of what had happened that morning. I did a good job on the brickwork and, after saying sorry a hundred times to the lady, she gave me £50. I think she felt sorry for me. I gave this money to Bernadette to keep her happy.

The next job we got was an Indian man in Belvedere, a lovely family. They owned the local DIY. The job was to plaster his bathroom. I put a whole bag of plaster into the bath and mixed it up and went for my breakfast next door to Andy's. After about an hour I returned to the bathroom and found that the whole bath had set. The man's wife came down with her two children to bath them to get them ready for school. She took one look at the bath, obviously now solid, and said could you please clean the bath out. It took me until four o'clock that day to clean it out. After I made another mess I decided to give up the building trade for good. London was in a deep recession and I had to sign on and take any work that I was offered to try to make ends meet. Bernadette had a swollen neck at this time and hyperactive glands. I don't think it was her fault but she was so angry all the time. Then one day a Dublin man came knocking at our door, Brendan. He used to do all the funerals with the priests, shaking the incense etc and he used to wear white clothes like the priests. He had nowhere to go so we let him stay on the couch for a few nights. I trusted him completely as I knew him from the church. Bernadette and I were going through a very difficult part of our married life. We had a lovely two-bedroomed house, which I had bought behind her back, and two lovely children. What was to happen took me completely by surprise, that she and Brendan had started a relationship. I asked them both what was going on. The betrayal really did hurt me. We had to go our separate ways and told him he could take my wife but over my dead body would he get my children. They set up home in Blackheath. We put our house on the market with an agreement everything split 50:50.

I was at that time, 1987-1988, working at St Margaret Clitherow RC School on a temporary basis while the school keeper was having a fourth bypass heart operation. I loved the school work and got on really well with the head teacher and staff, and most of all, I loved the children and got on really well with them. The school keeper was coming back in September after the summer holidays so I decided I would try and get a permanent job with a school that had a house with it. I applied for 17 jobs the first month without success. The council people who were doing the interviews got to know me. 'You do try, but you have not enough experience'.

Every night while I was working temporary at St Margaret before I locked up the school I would go over to our Lady of Lourdes statue and then rub the feet of St Margaret Clitherow's , stay about for ten minutes and ask for their help to get a job. I applied for a job at St Augustine's Primary School. There were eight applicants and the headmaster said, 'I will call out five names. You will please leave the building, three will remain. We will select from them'. My name was the first to be called. I knew I had not much of a chance as the same council men were on the panel that turned me down for previous jobs. I kept on trying and on the very last day of the summer term 1989 the house was sold, so the two girls and myself would have to go into a hotel. I cleared all the contents of our house into three skips I had hired. Burned every photo, every part of my life with Bernadette, threw all the furniture into the skips and smashed up almost everything that belonged to us. I had to be out the following Monday. I went to the Abbeymead for a pint worrying what I was going to do about the girls. Then Martin, the owner of the Club, came over to me to say the head teacher from St Augustine's was on the phone. Most of the staff at the school, including the lady head teacher from the infant school, had already left to go on their annual summer holidays. 'Mr Fahy have you had any job yet?' I said no. 'If you are still interested in St Augustine's meet me at the school Monday morning 9am. Don't be late as I am going to Australia and New Zealand on Monday'. I could not wait for the Monday and he told me he was so impressed by the head teacher's reference at St Margaret Clitherow he would take a chance with me. 'There's the keys of the school, and the keys to the house'. The man who got the job changed his mind at the last minute and I was the person living nearest the school. I felt elated as I started decorating and getting the house ready for use. I thanked Mr Mackney and told him I would do my best. There was one school for the junior children and a separate school for the infants. At first I was not sure I had the right job.

Bernadette left with Brendan and we were not to see her for another three years. From summer 1989 to 2005 I enjoyed St Augustine's. These were the happiest years of my life since I had come to London. I tried to give the girls the best I could, never once having an angry word with them, and basically let them do whatever they wished. The school was full then, almost 600 plus, and I got on really well with all the staff, and had a few favourites. I got on really well with all the children. In all my time there I never said or uttered an unfriendly word to any of them or to any of the staff. I was so grateful for the job and Bexley Council were brilliant in all their dealings with me. I was so sad when it finished. During my time at the school we had great relations with Father Roger and family at the church and playschool across the road, also with Father Peter. By 1991 Eileen had left school and Bernadette had moved on with Brendan. I think Eileen was a bit lonely not seeing her mum around. One day we were talking in the sitting room and she suddenly, out of the blue, said, 'Dad, we know all about mum's family, but we know nothing of yours'. I was shocked and could not answer, or was unable to speak. I promised her in 1991 I would go back to Ireland to see if I had any relatives. I did not even known what county I was born in.

I went to John and Hannah Coleman, 41 Connolly Road, and told them the position I was in. We had kept close contact over the years but I had not set foot in Ireland since 1965. They told me to go to John and Teresa's at Myrtleville in Crosshaven. They might be able to help me. John suggested going back to Upton first and the three of us set out early one morning to Upton in July 1991.

We met Father O'Sullivan who was in charge of Upton then and after a tour of Upton, he showed us books etc where my name was inscribed, also of beatings on me which also were logged. After a lovely dinner he had texted St Joseph's Clonmel and other places to see if they had any information on me, and promised he would do his best for me and let me know if anything came to light. As I looked around the school all the terrible memories of my childhood came flooding back to me. I wept openly. Father O'Sullivan had no knowledge of any family of me but said I had been born in St Anita's, Roscrea, Co Tipperary which was for unmarried mothers. I had to go back to London then but I could not wait to continue my search again.

In the summer of 1992, on the 15th of August, the Feast of the Assumption, I walked into church in Roscrea, after Mass, and spoke to the man who had served at the Mass and asked him if he knew of any Fahy's in the area. I still was not aware I was so close to St Anita's. He told me the bus to take and I arrived at St Anita's very self-guarded. Eventually I picked up courage and saw the Reverend Mother, a sister Hildergarde. She broke all the rules for me when I told her of my life to them and that I was looking for any connection to any relative. She showed me from a red book the record of my birth but it was sacred policy not to enter real mother's name as all mother's who gave birth there had to be protected. When I asked her about mums dying giving birth she told me she knew my mother personally as she was the youngest girl to give birth there. I think the actual age was 12 years 3 months. The other midwife Sister McCarthy I met in her retirement home in Herne Bay some years later. She did not die, and worked at St Anita's for two years until she was 14. The nuns at the Abbey had looked after me, and her, till the day my mother's father came for us. It was a big revelation to me. I went back and stayed in Myrtleville with John and Teresa. John promised that in summer 1993 he would find her, alive or dead. I returned to London full of hope and promise I would meet her one day.

I told the girls what had happened. 'Dad, don't go building you hopes up. Its fifty years ago. She is probably dead now'. I had to know, it was like an obsession with me by now. I went back to John and Teresa's in Myrtleville summer 1992, John ever so optimistic as usual. 'Paddy you might be very disappointed what you may find out. Are you sure you will accept what you find at St Anita's because of my birth there?' John said we would start there so he made a list of all the Fahy's. 'You stay in the car Paddy, I will do all the talking'. For hours we went here and there and all over Tipperary. We stopped at a shop in Cahir and John spoke to the lady whose daughter was also behind the counter. I was beginning to get agitated by now and it was raining very heavily. At about seven o'clock at night I said to John lets go back to Cork, forget all about it. John said 'Paddy, there's one more house I am going to try'. If that was no good we agreed to back to Myrtleville. As usual John went into the house and I stayed in the car. About 40 minutes went by. I knew at that moment that John had found something, or had information of some kind. It was still pouring with rain when John came back to the car. 'Paddy, get out'. As we walked back to the house an elegant lady was at the door. 'Julia, your son Paddy. Paddy your mother Julia'. He was like St John from the Gospel. I was overwhelmed and overjoyed. We embraced several minutes. I could not believe it. John said, 'I will wait in the car for you. As soon as you are ready'. We could not stop talking. Julia had married. David, Patrick, Christy and Catherine her children. Her husband, Con, was a lovely man, always respected me. John came back into the house and Julia made sandwiches.

I felt on top of the world as we drove back to Myrtleville that night. Teresa and John we so happy for me. I was full of euphoria and I could not wait to tell the girls of what had happened. Julia had been raped by a family friend at 11½ years old. After leaving the Abbey she looked after me, with her sisters Nell and Jude. The NSPCC thought I would be better off in an institution so while Julia was out working took me from Nell's arms and so I found myself in a nightmare that still badly hurts me and haunts me, even to this day and every day. I talked to Julia of the lady with the red coat and she said her father paid for it by 2/6 every week and bought it for her when she came home with me first.

When I arrived back in London I told the girls of what had happened. Julia was going to tell her children of me but sadly that was never to happen. I did get to see her when I went back for weekends with the Irish UN veterans and the ONET. We used to take over Tipperary Town for the weekend and I used to see Julia's children, sometimes grandchildren. Out of respect for her I could not let them know who I was. I used to see Christy, her youngest son and wife to be Marie. They used to have a caravan on the site while the extensions were being built. Christy only became aware of me in 2006 and David in 2007. When I saw the anger and hurt in David's face I knew I did not belong to this family. Julia had never told her children of me and could not bring herself to tell them. Julia has met my two daughters and has met Chloe and Shannon but has not met Kyla, Deirdre's daughter yet. The disappointment that I had not meant anything to her, or maybe the hurt she experienced the day the NSPCC had removed me from the family home is still too much a burden on her. I can only guess. She has seven sisters and seven brothers. Many I have already met, and their children. I have met most of their children, and after the initial meeting, even though I have left telephone calls and cards sent on numerous occasions, I never hear anything from them.

The only person who has invited me to her home and phones me on a regular basis is Kitty who lives in Orpington. Her family are very supportive to me. As I go into my last few years I do not, and cannot understand what a family is. I can only say for myself I always want to know where my daughters and granddaughters are. How they are doing and try to see them whenever possible. That is probably God's gift to me, and I am glad for the one reason maybe Julia would not have married and had four lovely children, and for that I accept what happened to me, was God's will and after what happened to Julie. She had a happy life afterwards. Whatever cross we have to bear in life though so difficult and hurtful to understand as we go through it. Its got to happen to somebody. I am so happy it happens to be me and not you, as I looked down on all the children during my work over twenty plus years in schools. I am glad it was not them but me it happened to. God bless.

Patrick at the tunnel entrance Elizabethville
Congo

Patriack in
Congo 1973

Patrick in Kilkee 1973

Mother Julie
Finchley
1947

Patrick Fahy

Arbour Hill Un Memorial

At the Cenotaph 2003

Chloe, Ilene, Patrick

Patrick at the Sheep Fold Bartres St. Bernadettes
Workplace

Congo Memorial Thurles, 2003 Patrick at the 3 right

Patrick at the second place at Taoiseach Bertie Ahern
UK ambassedor

John & Hanna at the Horse Shoe Pub

Chloe and Shannon at Christening

Chloe
Grandauther
at age 9

Deirdree & Kyla

Eileen & Shannon

Maiking Daisy Chain with Kyla

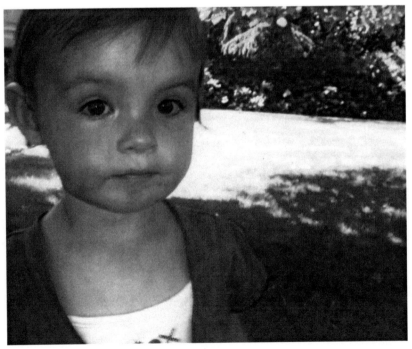

Kyla

The Sheep Fold Bartres

IN 2005 I MOVED TO 33 OVERTON ROAD, Abbey Wood from 68 St Augustine's Road, Belvedere. I miss St Augustine's, especially the children. Miss Trott, head teacher at St Margaret Clitherow RC School, Thamesmead offered me the job here as caretaker. I had done voluntary work there since I left on a temporary basis in 1988. I have had a lovely relationship with the school ever since. All through my time at St Augustine's I would go there and help in any way I could. One evening I am sitting at home when the phone rings. A lady I never heard from before, 'Could I have a few minutes of your time Patrick, I am your first cousin. My mother and your mother are sisters. Would you come over to Finchley and meet us?'

I went the following Saturday with Chloe my eldest granddaughter. Marie and her daughter Laura met us from the tube station. Marie drove us to her house where I met her husband, Manuel, her other daughters Mya and Rianna, and her mother Nell. I was so happy that morning. Marie and the children are so very beautiful. We were almost on a telephone call every day. I went to Mya's Confirmation, again with Chloe. Nell was the perfect aunt to me. She told me so much of family history and that the NSPCC had pulled me from her arms in 1944. I don't know how she found out about me or where she got my telephone number.

I almost felt Marie and me were of the same soul. I loved her and her family's company. When she decided would I like to go to Ireland with her and the girls, I was overjoyed. So we booked the trip. Nell decided at the last minute she would come as well. We would go to Julia's, my mother, house in Tipperary and also have a few days in Cork.

We went to Cork and stayed in Watergrasshill, a lovely place. We drove to Upton one morning and left Nell and the girls in Patrick Street, Cork to do shopping. Marie and I went down to Upton. As I had told her of my time I'd spent there she wanted to see for herself. We visited the Boys Cemetery, as one of my best friends had died there when he was twelve. I said a few prayers for him and for some of the priests and masters that were also buried there. We spent a few hours there and the staff were very courteous to us and let us walk freely around the school. It brought so many bad memories back to me. I said that would be my last visit. I had spent six and a half years there yet I could not remember even one happy moment during all that time. Marie took lots of photographs of Upton but I have not seen any of them yet.

We drove to Castle Freke, Rosscarbery, where I almost died as a ten year old. We went to Blarney Castle and I saw where my shoe shop was. Its still there. I went up to see Mrs Looney who was so good to me in my six months at Blarney. Then we went to Tipperary to see Nell's sister, Julia, my mother. After visiting John and Teresa O'Connor at Myrtleville I introduced Nell and Marie and told them this is the man that found Julia. We had a lovely supper and then we had a drink at Pine Lodge with John. I owe John and Teresa so much; I could never even begin to repay them.

We got to Julia's house, my mother, who put on a great lunch for us all. Then I met Julia's eldest son, David, who had never heard or knew of me. When Julia told David of me he was in a temper. He stands about 6ft 6ins, a builder. He said to Christy, 'Did you know of this?' Christy said, 'Only in the last year'. The hurt on his face then. I thought he was going to hit me. If he had, such a powerful man. I wanted to disappear into the earth with the embarrassment. I felt for my mother and myself. I knew I had no place in this family and it would hurt Julia all the more if I stayed a moment longer. I left the house then and booked myself into a B&B in Tipperary Town for that night. The next morning I went to Pauline's sister-in-law in Clontarf, Dublin. Pauline has always been a true friend and I would speak to her of anything. I may not have had a happy marriage but the sisters that Bernadette had have always been so good to me. I feel so ashamed I could not have been better and made Bernadette happy in her life.

Nell, Marie's mum, told me so much during the week to Cork and Marie, so beautiful and supportive in every way. I felt the hurt of not having a family slowly began to fade. We exchanged telephone calls on an almost daily basis. Then I met Carmel, Julia's brother's daughter. She lives in Hatfield. I have been over to see her a few times. John her husband got mugged and badly beaten on his way to a Chelsea match in 2006. I met Carmel's family and had a lovely dinner with them in a beautiful home. Then I met Kitty, another daughter of one of my mother's sisters. She has two daughters, Catherine and Elizabeth, and a son Matthew who is married to Lisa with a lovely baby Hannah. They all work at Queen Mary's Hospital, Sidcup. They are all so good to me. I never felt as comfortable or as welcome or at ease with anyone than Marie. At least I now have the family I craved for. Her lovely girls Laura, Mya and Rianna could not have treated me better and Manuel her husband a proper gentleman.

I went to Mya's Confirmation at her local church in Finchley. It was very special to me. I also went to Marie's 50th birthday party, a surprise party. My heart then reached for the stars. I think Marie has the same soul as me, as if we shared the same spirit. Then Marie's dad died in December 2007. All the communications stopped, no telephone calls, no answer to letters etc. I don't know who gave Marie the advice to sever the bond between us. I know it would never be Manuel or herself. To suddenly have so much love given to you and without warning it disappears in the same way. Its another arrow in your heart and you have to bear it as much as it hurts. Whoever gave this advice to Marie will one day have to explain that decision to God himself. I miss Marie and her family so much it hurts. I am now back to square one again, but Kitty and the girls keep in touch. I have my own two girls, Eileen and Deidre. Three lovely granddaughters, Chloe, Shannon and Kyle. That compensates for almost everything. I don't know if I will ever learn the truth from my family, of being the outcast. Deep down in my heart I do know, and I suppose the positive of this is my mother, married to a wonderful man, had three sons and one daughter, and had a happy life. For her I would not want it any other way. She went through so much hurt as a child herself. I did not write this script. Its written by God himself for whatever reason. I can't understand any of it but we are born for a reason and have to accept whatever comes our way in life without mercy or compassion.

I FIRST KNEW AND HEARD OF JULIA MY mother in 1991 as I had always believed her dead giving me birth. Sister Hildergarde at Sean Ross Abbey was so good to me. She asked me where and why I was not wearing any teeth. When I told her of what happened in Kilkenny and Upton, especially Upton, where you never had a dinner, only lumps of fat in hot water, as hungry as you were, it was uneatable. The malnutrition had set in at a very early age. We used to get salt of some kind to wash our teeth but by 30 years of age most of mine had fallen out. I bought several sets of teeth but within a few days my mouth would be full of ulcers and bleeding so I had to abandon that phase and go without teeth at all for nearly 30 years. My daughter, Deidre, threw the false sets out with the rubbish one day so that was the end of that problem. Sister Hildergarde took pity on me then. She broke all the rules. She took a big red book down from the shelf. I told her my birthday and she said she remembered my mother very well as she was one of the youngest, if indeed the youngest mother who was a patient there. She told me Sister McCarthy and herself helped deliver me and attended Julia, my mother, who was only 12 ¾ years old. Sister McCarthy lives in Herne Bay. Myself and Eileen, my eldest daughter, spent an afternoon and had dinner at her Convent. The nuns there were brilliant and I told them why I had come to visit them.

Sister Hildergarde then told me that I had spent my first two years with my mother at Sean Ross Abbey, and Julia had to work around the Abbey with me in tow. The nuns there loved me and I had about six mothers there. At 16 years Julia went back to Springfield Road with me. It was 1942 then and my mother was from a family of eight girls and seven boys. There were lots of children sent from London there. Because of the bombings in London it was a much safer place to be. From what I was to learn later in life there were about 12 children there. In March 1944 while Julia was out working the NSPCC removed me from Springfield Road, four years of age. The very moment I arrived at Kilkenny Orphanage, Kells Road, Kilkenny, I will never forget that moment. I have remembered it all through my life and I still hear the sound of the pony and trap. I remembered being helped down the steps of the trap and I was hungry and frozen with the cold. Because of my age I don't know how I coped then but on my hospital records I had spent my first two years very sick all the time and had spent a considerable time in hospital at St Luke's in Kilkenny.

In 1961 as I was about to embark with the 34th Irish Battalion to Congo and we were stationed at Collins Barracks, Dublin. I made enquiries and learnt she was working in a hospital in Dublin. I decided I would visit her as I wanted to see the person who had given me such a beating. I went up there in full Irish army uniform. No problem getting to meet her. As I saw this frail lady coming towards me I only felt sorrow and pity. I never said anything about the beating. She gave me a set of Rosary beads and scapular to take with me to the Congo. I never saw her again.

I remember sitting on a round stone near a river, lots of the other children were there and I think we had lots of children from St Joseph's the girls school in Kilkenny. While in Kilkenny and Upton lots of mums used to come back to take children out. I had a special friend, Tom Nugent. Tom was from Waterford. His mum came back a few times to see him. He always shared whatever his mum gave him with me. Then one day Tom was gone forever. Then I had another best friend Martin Ryan. Sadly Martin died when he was twelve. I still remember his red hair. He was buried in the Boys Graveyard. I still remember his funeral, his white coffin. Then one of the priests died,

Father Noonan. It was the first person I saw dead. He lay in bed with brown clothes and a big Rosary bead in his hands.

Then Upton passed on, my army years, my twenty years working in London on the buildings. Especially when I was working for classics swimming pools. I worked for a lot of high profile people including Freddie Mercury at his house in Brompton Road and John Taylor from Duran Duran. I worked at most coastal Health Centres putting in Jacuzzis and miniature swimming pools. I would have to dig out most by hand. All I would have on was my underpants and a pair of Wellies and the temperatures in these places would be 100+. Then I moved into school's quite by accident. My local Parish Priest was looking for someone to cover the Local Roman Catholic School during the Christmas holidays. I went in for two weeks and worked in the school's for the last 23 years.

In 1991 Eileen, my eldest girl, asked me if I had any family. She wanted to know them, which was her right. I went back to Ireland the summer term of 1991 and went to Crosshaven where I met Teresa and John. I had not been back in Ireland since leaving Ireland in 1965. Although I had been to Kilkee a few times with Bernadette I had never been back to Cork. Teresa and John let me stay at their villa in Myrtleville, Crosshaven. I told them I had to find out if I had any living relatives in Ireland. John said what county are you from Paddy. I answered him I don't know so he said to me we will make a start with Upton where you went to school. John and Teresa helped me pay all my expenses and John drove us to Upton.

Father O'Sullivan was in charge of Upton then. He opened a bottle of whiskey and drinks etc, plus a lovely dinner. We were treated as VIP. He told us to go to Sean Ross Abbey, Roscrea, Tipperary which used to be a place for unmarried mums; it is now for the mentally and physically handicapped children. He could not help us any further. After about five hours in Upton, he showed us books. My name was entered in several pages from beatings that were administered for whatever reasons by the Brothers. I do know the terrible memories of those years came flooding back to me and I cried openly. We left Upton as I had to go back to London that week. I wrote to the Abbey at Roscrea. I went back there 1992 summer term. Then I learned the awful truth that my mother was still alive and still lived in the same house. In 1993 John was still helping me and we eventually made contact with Julie, my mother.

It was euphoria for me as we drove back to Myrtleville that night. John, Teresa and myself went to the Crosshaven Rugby Football Club that night. We celebrated until three o'clock that morning. Teresa was so happy for me. I thanked John for what he and Teresa had done for me. I could not wait to tell my daughters Eileen and Deirdre. I met my mother, she was going to tell her children of me but she could not face the problem or tell any of her children of me. To find your own mother but to be then treated as a family outcast. Year after year I made all the running to try to be part of my family. I would be visiting Tipperary with the Irish UN veterans and ONET. I might spend half an hour with Julia. Sometimes I would go to the Abbey by the bridge and see if her bicycle was under the stairs. That was the best and only communication I was offered.

All what happened to me in 1944 was told to me by Sean Ross Abbey, or a few people I have known from my time in the army. I learned Julia had me; she was raped at 12 and I was born March 1940. I learnt the man who did the rape was never prosecuted but I learnt where his family are now living, and his son and their whereabouts. I have visited the town to see for myself what sort of a family they were, and are. I kept this from everyone and never told anyone of knowing the identity. Julia's youngest son and wife have always treated me well, as did her husband who could not have been kinder to me during this difficult time. Julia married and has three boys and a girl. Since 1991 I have seen them many times with their children. It was like I was invisible. I could see them but they could not see me. I stood bedside Christy, the youngest boy, I knew who he was but he didn't know me. I would never blame Julia for any hurt I suffered as she was only a child herself when she had me and I think now the NSPCC maybe were right in taking me away. All I know from that moment I was taken from Nell's arms, Julia's sister, I would be damaged forever and could never recover. What is life worth if you never ever receive any love from your mother or your own family? To be totally abandoned by your own mother and seven aunts and seven uncles, knowing you were sent to such places as Kilkenny and Upton and nobody ever made an enquiry about you. I went on holiday with Nell, Julia's sister, and her daughters and granddaughters in 2007.

During this holiday Julia was trying her best to set me back into the fold but David was so outraged at finding out about me. I felt at that moment so much pity and sorrow for Julia. I quit the scene and vowed I would never ever go back to that house again. Julia will probably live there till she dies. I try to understand why no-one ever tried to make contact with me. I have lived almost seventy years of age yet the yearning to belong to something, or somebody, or some family, still haunts me. Nell often used to say I was tempted to go back for you but I did not, nor did any of her brothers and sisters.

I battled for 16 years with the NSPCC as to why I was taken away from my family. With help from HM The Queen, who is Patron, I got a full apology from them for their part in this. Maybe it was God's will that Julia would meet such a lovely man as her husband, have four wonderful children and a wonderful life. I do not begrudge her any of that and am glad she found such a lovely man. I don't know what is the worse, losing your mother at four years of age or finding her in August 1993, and then realise your past history and be ashamed of you. I wish I had not gone on the trip in 1991 to 1993 then I would not have that extra hurt I have to this day.

MY NAME IS PATRICK. I WAS BORN in March so Patrick was the obvious choice, as St Patrick is March 17th, and St Joseph March 19th my second name was Joseph. As I have written I experienced a childhood so terrible that you never ever could recover even part of the damage bestowed upon you. I never even knew that everyone had a mother until I reached 12 years of age when my best friend, Tom, was taken from Upton. His mother said to me you have a mother too Paddy. She might come and get you out as well. She gave me sweets and I said goodbye to Tom; I never saw him again. I never knew that everybody had a mother until that moment. I remember my time in Kilkenny, St Patrick's, Kells Road and also at St Patrick's, Upton. I could not understand why some of the boys went on holiday for summer holidays and some of us went on holiday camp with the Brothers. To be fair during this month the Brothers treated us much better than in the other eleven months. We used to go on holidays to Garrettstown to a great big house owned by some charity.

After Upton I joined the Irish Army for six years with a broken leg I had endured with farmers in Co Kerry who had been given permission to employ me by the Irish Children's Society. I was a shoe repairer and general labourer and then I moved to England in 1965 to forget my childhood and everything of Ireland.

I got married to a Co Clare girl named Bernadette. It was not founded on love so it was a disaster from day one. We just did not gel. We did have two lovely girls, Eileen and Deidre and I feel I am very close to them. Eileen has two daughters and Deidre has one. I worked in London mostly on building sites and a few years doing swimming pools etc during which I met a lot of famous people.

I met my mother Julia after nearly 50 years since I was led to believe she had died giving me birth. The heartache before I met her in 1993 was to continue to the present day, 2008, as she could not bring herself to tell her children of me. I was such an embarrassment to everyone, and to the family. I had my last 23 years working in schools. I loved that work and got on great with the children. I was at the local park the other morning with Deidre and while we were pushing Kyla on the swing she turned to me and said, 'Dad if I were to lose Kyla, she is 16 months old, I would die. Now I understand what you have been trying to say to me for years. I just can't imagine me without Kyla, or Kyla without me. I would be worried every minute of what she was doing, if she was hungry or if anything was the matter with her. I feel so sorry for you'. That statement just about sums up everything. I could and would not abandon my children. I reared them both for three years on my own.

During my time on the building I felt at sometimes I had physic powers. I worked on six buildings that collapsed and on three or more times I had persuaded the men to come down the ladder before the collapse. One day I had phoned Albills several times that day who supplied the concrete pumps that poured the concrete as I had fears of a collapse that day. They told me to do what I was paid for. I told the site agent of my fear and he said I was a thick Paddy. I was working with Peter Flynn, a next door neighbour of Mr Stevens who owned Albills. I told Peter that day of my concern and he told him to stay off the building that day. We had about 90 metres of concrete poured and the whole decking collapsed as we were washing out the pump and pipes. They took notice of me after that. I was working at Catford another day and I got six men down after a similar fear. The last man had just gone down when that decking also collapsed. They used to say I put the mockers on the pours. I knew somebody somewhere was watching over me. I just got this gut feeling when something seemed of danger. Like the times in the Congo I felt all through my life that in spite of everything I had a guardian angle or something, or someone I could not understand looking after me. There were several times this had happened to me. No doubt these warnings saved other lives too.

I try to understand my life, what and why my mother and I had to part. We can be in a room now but we don't respond with a kiss or a hug, just emptiness and sorrow. I feel the education I received as a child was so poor and inadequate. I never had a chance whatsoever in life itself. I did not know but sex was taboo and it was considered a mortal sin to ask about it. It wasn't until I was about 29 years old and I told the girl I was going out with I had never had sex, or I never knew anything of sex. She did offer masturbation for me and that was my first ever understanding of sex. I feel sorry for Helen and Kathleen who I had gone out with, all the other girls as well. I was totally ignorant of everything sexual. I have been on my own, apart from the 18 years with Bernadette. I did try my best for her. I think because I never knew love myself I could not give it to her the way she desired. Maybe that was why she left us. I say I am sorry for anyone I may have done wrong to, or hurt in anyway. I just hope another child does not have my life.

IRELAND AND THE REDRESS
BOARD

AN APOLOGY BY THE TAOISEACH, AND THE SETTING up of a System of Redress, to the children of Ireland, who lost their childhood years, to sometimes brutal and cruel regimes, who suffered so much, in what should have been their happiest days turned to the most horrific days of their childhood memories. Many of these children like me, are in their late 60s and 70s. What our memories are belong to an Ireland so cruel, most of us, would have left it in our 20s. Campaigners who were sincere in getting Redress for these victims of such obscene child abuse.

When I have told friends and people I worked with in London of my own childhood experiences, they say it could not be possible. I weep to myself because, in their lives, it just could not, and would not happen. But it did happen to us and even though I am one of the many victims I feel ashamed to be part of our country's blackest history. To leave your own children down to such appalling depths of despair, be it family or country, is the most evil bottomless pit you can descend into.

While Mr Ahern, and his Party, have admitted its past Government's failures, the Redress System it set up was to be more beneficial to the solicitors bank accounts than it was meant to. As in most cases of dealing with justice, most of the allocated money for Redress was spent on the hiring of buildings and solicitors, and not where the genuine people, who campaigned for justice for these children, had intended to go. I doubt that any other country in the world would have the courage to put up its hands and say we got it so wrong, and they did try somehow to make amends.

The Redress System has helped me and my family. But why it happened nobody seems to know. How when I left Upton at 16 years of age, the Brothers must have known my mother was still alive and living in the same house I was abducted from and still lives there. Why was I not told at that age? I could have rebuilt a family life. No, they chose to tell me my mother had died giving me birth, and it would be nearly fifty years later on I would find out she was very much alive. She was told that I also had died. I just don't understand any of it to this day. But why?

A letter from me Monday 17 January 2004

68 St Augustines Road
Belvedere
Kent DA17 5HH

0208 311 2956

Dear Taoiseach

Mr Ahern

I have written to your office before and I would like to say a sincere 'thank you', and to all your Government, who did so much work on behalf of people who had spent their childhood life in an institution for whatever reason.
I met you in person at the GAA Ground in Ruislip. I was one of your Guard's of Honour. You

yourself have enhanced the very Proclamation of Ireland, by reaching out to Ireland's most unwanted, uncared and most unloved children, and have reached out to us, who live hundreds of miles from Ireland.

I received £57,000 sterling from the Redress Board. My eldest daughter, Eileen, has two daughters, Chloe 10, Shannon 6. £13,000 I gave to Eileen as Shannon has cerebral palsy. It has secured a better life for Shannon, as she has to have 24 hours a day care. To my other daughter Deidre, £13,000. She has put a deposit on her first own home, so it has been a big lift for her. £1,500 to a widowed mother with two small children, their first holiday in Spain for five years and also a family in my school, £1,000 who never ever had a holiday. As for myself £17,000 I have invested. I had debts of £4,000 which I could never ever repay, and my children would be left with the debt. I have repaid all my debts, got new clothes, and am now looking forward to retirement 8 March '05. So to the Redress Board, and solicitor and to all the legal people, who made it all happen, thank you all. It certainly has helped me. But it was your own courage and taking the stand in the Dail that made it happen.

On behalf of my two daughters and two granddaughters, I thank you and Ireland. I don't think any other leader of Government in the world would have done so and that's what make us love Ireland, if it was possible, all the more.

Yours sincerely

Patrick P Fahy

No 806799 34-36-39 Battalions, Congo

I ARRIVED IN CORK 10TH DAY OF JUNE 2008. It was lovely to be back in Cork City again to see St Patrick's Bridge and Street and to hear the wonderful bells of Shandon ringing out over the City. I visited the Lough near Ballyphehane before going out to Connolly Road to see a great friend Finn Barr.

On Wednesday I visited Barry and Sheila at Tower, Blarney after a visit to the castle and a visit to the lakes in the woods, where Ray and I used to go fishing. No place in the world could possibly have this enchantment. Its so peaceful you could only hear the birds and not meet another person until you actually left the woods itself.

On Thursday 12 June, I spent the day in Dublin. Visited Collins Barracks Museum and the United Nations Memorial at Arbour Hill. I love Dublin City Centre. I always think of it as the Heart of Ireland. I had a lovely meal in the Yatch Club in Clontarf, then I walked out to the Lady of the Sea (statue) along the coastal walk of Clontarf. You can see this statue, lit up at night, to guide the British ferries into Dublin safely. Then back to Clontarf Hotel to watch Euro 2008, and a few pints. The following morning I had to be up early to go to Kilkenny. I had not been there since 1949. I wonder if it's still the same as in my memory.

I arrived in Kilkenny City by coach, and then I got a taxi to the gates of Kilkenny Convent. The gateway and entrance, and the trees lining the avenue were exactly as I remembered them. The huge stone clad building and the statue of the Sacred Heart and Mary were the exact as in my memory. I met Sister Joan O'Neill. She told me the Reverend Mother was very poorly. I had a lovely dinner given to me, salmon mash, wild potatoes, carrots and peas, all served by a beautiful lady.

Sister Mary Imelda is 88 years old and is not able to see any visitors today. After dinner Sister Joan took me to the nuns cemetery. I had remembered one of the Sisters being buried there during my time at the Convent. I said her name. She said to me, 'You have a great memory'. I then said to her, 'I also went to another graveyard further up'. She said, 'that's the Boys Graveyard'. I told her I had been there at a funeral during my time. There again I was spot on. It was in a disused meadow in the very corner of the field as we walked through the graveyard where row after row of children, back as far as the 1800 hundreds, are buried. They had no family contact and only the Sisters and the children come to pray for them.

I had spent a lot of my time at St Luke's Hospital Kilkenny during 1944, 1945 and 1946 and received the last rites in 1950. I thought if I had died during this period of my life I would also have been buried here. Not a worldly person would have known, or cared. I felt tears in my eyes as I surveyed everything. I kept my feelings inside as I did not want to upset the lovely Sister. She spoke of the children with so much love. I knew I was in the presence of someone special, and of God himself.

The abandoned children of someone, somewhere all lie here, forgotten by generations. Only the Sisters that work here visit these lonely graves. I could so easily have been one of them. I had planned that very evening on visiting my mother in Tipperary but this visit changed things. I left Kilkenny about 4pm and thanked the lovely Sister for her kindness to me. We never stopped talking all the time. The place had so many memories for me, including my first Holy Communion Day. Some of the children had family come to see them on this special day. No one arrived for me.

I arrived in Dublin about 7pm. I met my sisters-in-laws, Pauline and Doris, and Pauline's son Roger. I told them I would travel down to Tipperary the next morning and I phoned my mother to tell her. I would be arriving later on. I said goodbye to Pauline's family the next morning and started on my journey down to Tipperary at Limerick Junction.

I did not feel comfortable by calling to my mother as I remembered what happened the year just before and the memory of Kilkenny still fresh in my mind. If I had died I would be forever a part of that disused meadow. No family member would have even known where I lay. I decided then and there I would not go where I am not wanted and took the coach back to Cork.

I love Cork so much. I felt happy and at ease again. By calling to my mother I felt I would be hurting her more by my presence, and in front of her grandchildren and her family, trying to explain me to them. I have to let go of the mother I had just until four years of age, through no fault of her, or me. We lost one another then and I suppose in reality it was to be forever, though I did try and revive the situation. It was hopeless and the prayers I have said for a complete reunion might go to somebody else in a similar situation. I have always felt great sorrow for my mother as she was just a very young child herself when she had me. We both had to suffer. When the final hour comes maybe it may rekindle something of those early years. No-one knows what happens when we finally leave this world.

I have had many memories while in Kilkenny and Upton afterwards of somebody very close to me with a red coat. I was to learn afterwards that this lady was someone very special.

I first knew that something was wrong as I arrived at Kilkenny orphanage at Kells Road, Kilkenny. I was frozen with the cold and hungry, and had the inner feeling of something happening that was not good for me. I heard the pony and trap stopping, someone helping me down the steps of the trap. I still remember that exact moment as if its happening just this moment.

I remember standing underneath the Statue of the Sacred Heart on my Holy Communion Day. Your first Holy Communion is always a special day in any child's life. I had a red silk badge with a medal on it. During my time in Kilkenny I spent quite a lot of time in St Luke's, Kilkenny.

During 1944, 1945, 1946 and 1950 I had almost died. I don't know if this was because I was removed from my family or not, I don't know, but I always understood my mother had died giving me birth and I always believed it to be true, and I did not doubt for a minute that this indeed had happened.

I think the nuns at Kilkenny did their best for us but I do recall eating the leaves and the pink blossoms from the trees. I knew most of the wild plants that grew and the one's which were nicer to eat. I always seemed to be hungry. I do recall one lovely nun, I think her name was Sister Philomena. I used to help her and I remember her always being good and kind to me. She used to work in the laundry. I think one of the Sister's and two of the boys died during my time in Kilkenny. I know I had some happy days in Kilkenny and had mixed feelings when I left in 1949.

I was met by a Brother Ryan at Kilkenny bus station. I was with another boy Roger Doyle. We arrived at Brians Cross about two and a half miles from Upton Industrial School. We walked rough roads and dirt boreens. It was raining as we arrived at the main gates of the school, St Patrick's Industrial School, Upton, Co Cork. The Brother hardly spoke a word all through the journey. We went up a big avenue that seemed to go on forever. The Boys Graveyard was on the right-hand side as you went towards the school. Only the ducks and hens were in view as you got nearer the school. Then we passed the cowshed and farm itself, and the boiler house.

The Brother then bought us into the kitchen where we were given bread and butter and jam and tea. We were taken to the dormitory and shown where we were to sleep. If I had known what I was to experience over the next six years I would have preferred death a hundred times. Life in Upton must have been designed by Satan himself.

The children from the big cities of Ireland who had been caught stealing, or not attending school, were sent to Upton as punishment. Most were from Dublin. The Brothers then made these children Prefects in charge of us who had no mums or dads. I would receive beatings almost on a daily basis. There was no one to tell your problems to, you lived in total fear and you were ruled by total fear. There was never a hint of love from anyone. I used to wet my bed almost nightly. In the morning you had to carry your mattress to the boiler house. The man in charge of the boiler house would put it on top of the boiler range to dry the wet mattress. Then after school you would have to carry it back again to the dormitory in front of the other children who would laugh at you and call you 'slashers'. I did visit the boiler house on a daily basis until I was nearly fourteen years of age, despite the night watchman, Mr Roe, getting us up for two visits during the night. If you did not get up immediately you would get his walking stick a few times across your bum and back. Then you had to queue up, as there was only two toilets for nearly 100 children.

The children in spring had to plant all the crops and then the thinning. Then in the autumn the reaping, picking the potatoes, pulling the flax, mostly supervised by civilian farmers hired by the school. The work was back-breaking. You had no choice but to do what you were told. If you did not do what you were told you would be in for a hiding. At 14 years of age I was sent to the Boot & Shoe Trade shop, as we had to learn a trade before leaving the school.

As written from The Irish History Archives

As it turned out, the advice of de Valera, who of course had seen military action during the 1916 rising, proved to be of more value than the archbishop's. Few people could have believed that within four months thousands of people would again line the streets of the Capital, but this time to pay homage to the Irish victims of a massacre in the Congo.

The tragedy struck on 8 November 1960 near the village of Niemba in Katanga, when an eleven-man Irish patrol was ambushed by Baluba tribesmen at a river crossing. The Irish had been sent out to repair a bridge that the Baluba had destroyed the previous day to halt incursions into their territory by Katangan troops. The Baluba of northern Katanga were loyal to the central government in Léopoldville and, thus, were opposed to Katangan President Moise Tshombe's secessionist forces. Eight members of the Irish patrol died at the scene, hit by a hail of arrows. Some were bludgeoned to death as they lay wounded. Others died within minutes from the effect of poison on the arrow tips. Not all the arrows were poisoned but those that were had been dipped in the deadly venom of the Black Mamba snake. Approximately 25 Baluba were killed in return fire. Three Irish soldiers managed to escape. Two of these, Tom Kenny and Joe Fitzpatrick, were found alive a few days later in a search operation. But the search parties failed to find the third man,

Anthony Browne, who was initially listed as 'missing, presumed dead'.

To this day, there are conflicting accounts of the ambush, date and location of Trooper Browne's death. He is officially listed by the army as having died at the scene of the massacre. In addition, the citation for the military medal for gallantry awarded to him in September 1961 (he was the first recipient of this, the army's highest honour) reads: 'He endeavoured to create an opportunity to allow an injured comrade to escape by firing his Gustaf thereby drawing attention to his own position which he must have been aware would endanger his life. He had a reasonable opportunity to escape because he was not wounded but chose to remain with an injured comrade'. The citation infers that Browne did not escape the scene, but perished there.

However, the Trooper Browne story did not end there. In late 1962 the army learned from a Belgian lawyer in Elizabethville, the capital of the province of Katanga, that Browne's remains had been discovered. A search party of Irish troops were detailed to recover the body, travelling to the area on 5 November and recovering the remains on 7 November. The army's four-page report of this operation, entitled 'Recovery of remains of Trooper Browne in the Niemba area, 5/7 November 62' contains a map showing that the soldier's body was found almost three miles from the massacre site.

As more facts emerged about what had really happened to Trooper Browne, the 33rd Battalion's unit history had to be amended in late 1962. An appendix to the Battalion's unit history states: 'Information which we had received from Baluba survivors [of the 8 November 1960 incident in Niemba] in Manono hospital led us to believe that he [Browne] had been killed immediately after saving Private Kenny, and that his body had been removed from the scene by the ambushers'. After explaining how Browne's body was discovered two years after the ambush, army officials added the following wording in the appendix: 'Apparently some days after the ambush, wounded, exhausted and starving he [Browne] had called some women at the outskirts of the village [of Tundulu] and asked them for food and directions to the railway line, offering them 200 francs. They took the money but instead of helping him they told the young men of the village who came out and killed him'.

Brigadier-General PD Hogan was in charge of the Niemba search party in November 1960. In the last interview given before his death in Cyprus in March 2004, the retired general admitted that Browne had survived the ambush only to be killed by tribesmen 'some days later' having 'travelled some miles through the bush'. Hogan added this personal view of the Niemba tragedy:

CONCLUSION

I **RECEIVED A LETTER FROM MY MOTHER,** which beyond, all doubt proves the documents entered by both NSPCC and the circuit judge of Tipperary SR Colnmel, had both been entered on my behalf false. These were both acts of perjury. Been carried out by people who we believe are supposed to be for the care of the child. I have had a letter of apology from the NSPCC which most of, I do not agree with at all. How can any justification that a child's imprisonment for nearly 14 years is accepted as the norm of the day, what utter and ridiculous nonsense of such a statement is this. While the patron of the NSPCC, H.M. The Queen gave me such uplifting support, and it was only on her authority, I received an apology at all, I think, that in all child societies, there should be an independent government body monitoring their every move. I am only one child, how many more have suffered the same fate as I have done. There are always those in authority that do not care for the children, but of their own personal needs that came first. I also read a letter from Friar Joseph O' Reilly, which I fully know came from his heart and which I accept fully, also a letter from my mother Julia and a letter from her sister Nell. I don't know the human boundary, what the bond of a mother and child is, or should be, I have missed the bond since my removal, nearly 64 years ago, to today in 2008. I know the difficulty or think I do, what pain she also went though over the years. I have been alone in my heart and soul and reading through my hospital records, cant explain why I had to keep going back to hospital as from what I believe it was never of the physical kind, I had a great friend in my life, William Clements, he convinced me to work in the schools, he used to say to me, Pat, work for the children, they are nearest to god and by working with them and for them so will you be close to god.

Patrick Fahy

ABOUT THE AUTHOR

Born on the 4th March 1940 my name is Patrick Joseph Fahy. From 4 years old until I was 9 ½ old I spent most of my youth in religious establishments.

At St Patricks Kells Road Kilkenny, from what I remember of this time, I think on the whole, the Sisters here did their best for us. Although I do remember a beating so bad it locked in my mind for years after. It may be that I did something really bad, that I deserved it, as I don't think Sisters would have carried out a punishment like this for no reason. Maybe it was the only time I was beaten, during this period and was shocked by it. I accept it may be that reason.

The pain was as such that I cried enough tears to fill The Liffey, The Lee and The Shannon Rivers.

During my life I worked as a shoemaker, farmer, soldier, swimming pool and Jacuzzi builder, a bricklayer, a concrete pump operator, artex operative, a painter and for the last 20 years as a school caretaker and this was the best job of all. I used to see the mums and dads picking their children up after school each day and a kiss and a hug shared, it was just a reminder to me of what I missed and a tear would fill my eyes. As I still remember the smell and love of a lady in a red coat, that memory is with me to this day. Such memories fade as the years go on and are replaced by despair and acceptance that you are unloved and unwanted by anyone.

I never had education and did not know of the facts of life till I reached the age of 30. I was not aware of any sexual feelings until I was 29 years old and did not know of a lady's period time, till my wife was pregnant. Such was my ignorance, my wife thought I was joking, but I was not. My wife left me after 18 years together. I do not blame her at all as I was never a complete person and probably never will be. I just could not piece anything together. The last few years, thanks to my parish priest, I have gone to Lourdes several times and there in the Sheepfold at Bartres I identify someone who at 13 also worked as a child. I really find peace here and talk to Bernadette as if she is beside me.

Patrick j Fahy

Lightning Source UK Ltd.
Milton Keynes UK
19 October 2009